AMERICAN-
AUSTRALIAN
RELATIONS

by

WERNER LEVI

Assistant Professor of Political Science
University of Minnesota

UNIVERSITY OF MINNESOTA PRESS, MINNEAPOLIS

LONDON • GEOFFREY CUMBERLEGE • OXFORD UNIVERSITY PRESS

PRINTED AT THE COLWELL PRESS, INC., MINNEAPOLIS

Table of Contents

CHAPTER I

The First Contacts

THE United States of America initiated its Far Eastern trade in February 1784, when the *Empress of China* under Captain Green left New York for Canton. Many other ships soon followed in her wake, and in 1789 fifteen United States vessels were in Canton.[1] They usually sailed by way of Cape Verde, the Cape of Good Hope, and the Strait of Sunda, but sailing conditions were such that this route could be used only during the spring. This was a serious handicap to extensive and regular trade, and quite unsatisfactory to the owner of the *Empress of China*, Robert Morris. He decided to try another route.

On June 20, 1787, he dispatched his ship *Alliance* under Captain Reed from the Delaware River via the Cape of New Holland, as Australia was then called. It was a hazardous undertaking; no other ship had ever tried this passage before and sailing conditions were unknown. Captain Reed was provided only with a map of the world. But the trip proved successful. Without dropping anchor en route the *Alliance* arrived safely in Canton on December 22, 1787. The European captains there were amazed at this out-of-season arrival of the Americans. The event was so revolutionary that the British Admiralty became interested in it and made inquiries about the voyage.[2]

For the first time an American ship had sailed the Tasman Sea. There was no colony then in Australia; it was not established until one month later, in January 1788. The significance

[1] *Hunt's Merchant's Magazine*, IV:468 (1841). This chapter appeared first as an article in the *Pacific Historical Review*, XII:351 (1943).

[2] Letters of Phineas Bond, *Annual Report* of the American Historical Association, I:578 (1896); John Sanderson, *Biography of the Signers to the Declaration of Independence* (Philadelphia, 1828), II:431; Kenneth E. Latourette, "Early Relations between the United States and China," *Transactions* of the Connecticut Academy of Arts and Science, XXI:16, 45 (1917).

of the trip lay in the discovery of a new trade route to China. But it was clear that through the use of this route commercial intercourse with American traders was bound to begin, once a settlement was established in Australia. The plans of the British government for the colonization of "New Holland" were known to Americans and were eagerly watched. Even before the first settlers arrived at Botany Bay, Major Samuel Shaw, the first American consul in Canton, remarked that the colony "may become an important settlement, especially when it is remembered that mighty Rome had a similar origin."[3] His task was to discover trade possibilities and to stimulate interest in them, and neither he nor his friends and associates, the New England merchants, lost any opportunity for commerce in the Pacific. Hardly had the colony been founded in New South Wales when the first American ship arrived.

In 1791 Captain Thomas Patrickson, on a trip to China, had met in Cape Town Philip Gidley King, a member of Captain James Cook's crew and later governor of New South Wales. King told the captain about the new colony and suggested to him that a mixed cargo might be sold profitably there.[4] Little did King suspect what difficulties he was creating for himself with this advice. The following March Patrickson sailed from Philadelphia as master of the *Philadelphia* and arrived in Port Jackson on November 1, 1792, provided with a letter of recommendation to the governor, Phillip, by the British minister to the United States, Phineas Bond.[5]

The ship "had a cargo of assorted notions much needed in the settlement, and the speculative skipper sold the lot at a high figure, in addition to which he found employment for his ship between Sydney and Norfolk island in the transport of stores."[6] The assorted notions consisted of beef, pitch, tar, tobacco, gin, and rum. The "high figure" was £2829.11.—for

[3] Josiah Quincy, ed., *The Journals of Major Samuel Shaw* (Boston, 1847), 250.

[4] George Mackaness, *Admiral Arthur Phillip* (Sydney, 1937), 397.

[5] For another early American ship, see Roderick Flanagan, *The History of New South Wales* (London, 1862), I:81.

[6] From a manuscript quoted in a letter to the writer from the Royal Australian Historical Society, dated February 13, 1941.

the beef, pitch, and tar, which were bought by the colonial administration. The more profitable remainder of the cargo was bought at an undisclosed figure by the army officers for resale to the population.[7]

Governor Phillip bought the *Philadelphia* and she never returned to America. Her captain, Patrickson, went to England and secured a contract from the British government for transporting convicts to Australia.

Thus began a trade relation which proved beneficial to the American shipper but detrimental to New South Wales—because the cargo that American ships brought to Australia consisted to a very large extent of spirits. This was nothing novel to the New England exporter. Trading in Newfoundland for fish, in Guinea for gold, in the southern colonies for ships' stores, on the Northwest Coast for lumber, he had learned to appreciate his rum as an internationally welcome commodity.[8] It was no different in New South Wales.

Indeed, the clientele in the colony was most receptive. The colonists were not picked for their character. They were convicts sent to New South Wales from Great Britain as a punishment, and a large contingent of their guardians from 1792 on were soldiers released from military prisons for the purpose of controlling the young colony. Governor Macquarie reported home in 1812 that "the Nature of the Inhabitants of this Country is such that Spirits Must be had."[9]

The Americans (together with the British) provided them in abundance. The proportion of spirits to provisions in their cargoes grew larger and larger. One of the main reasons why the ships carried any other cargo at all was that foodstuffs and useful articles were convenient means of forcing the colonial administration to permit the landing of spirits too. Often the colony suffered from shortages of necessary provisions, and the arrival of an American ship with the needed supplies

[7] Mackaness, *Admiral Arthur Phillip*, 397.

[8] Charles W. Taussig, *Rum, Romance and Rebellion* (New York, 1928), 16.

[9] Parliament of Australia, Joint Library Committee, *Historical Records of Australia* (Sydney, 1914–   ), ser. 1, vii:593. The source will be cited hereafter as *HRA*.

was then most welcome. When the second American ship to Australia, the *Hope* under Benjamin Page, arrived on December 24, 1792, Lieutenant-Governor Grose examined the inventory of the commissary. He found it very small, and this fact, together with fear of a drought, made him decide to buy the provisions. But "I lamented on this occasion being obliged to purchase the spirits, without which he would not agree to the disposal of his provisions," Grose wrote to London.[10]

A few years later, in 1802, the colony's reserves of salted meat were dwindling. The timely arrival of the American ship *Arthur* with a quantity of meat, other supplies, and spirits saved the situation. The spirits were landed with the provisions, and Governor King had to purchase both, although he was "loth to direct any purchase from strangers."[11] Obviously, this kind of American trade was not favored with the governor's sympathy. The importation of these large quantities of spirits considerably affected the colony's development in the early years of its existence, and the effects could be noticed for many decades.

Under the governorship of Grose, from 1792 to 1794, the military succeeded in establishing complete dominance in New South Wales. Grose not only was unable to restrain the officers; he was actually their tool. They controlled the political and economic life of the settlement and used this control to further their own personal welfare by every means. Spirits played an important role in their domination of the population. They bought them at reasonable prices from the Americans and sold them at figures often reaching twenty times the purchase price.[12] It came to be a rule that provisions and other supplies of the American cargoes were bought by the commissary, and that the spirits were bought by the army officers.[13] In many cases, the whole cargo was bought up by the officers. If the populace ran out of cash with which to buy the

[10] *Ibid.*, ser. 1, I:413.

[11] *Ibid.*, III:600.

[12] *Cambridge History of the British Empire* (Cambridge, 1933), VII, pt. I, "Australia," 72.

[13] *HRA*, ser. 1, II:681; V:167.

spirits, they paid for them with their labor or the products of their labor. In many instances spirits replaced currency. Seemingly the only thing of value to the inhabitants of the settlement at that time was spirits.

The worst effect of the situation was that the governor was entirely in the hands of the officers. They obtained from him huge grants of land, which they worked with convict labor or with free settlers who had gone into the officers' debt through the purchase of liquor. The whole structure of the New South Wales economy was thus changed. The plan, as originally conceived by the British government, to develop an economy of large public and small private farming was disregarded. Instead, a monopoly economy with the military clique as landowners arose.

Grose's equally incapable successor, Paterson, did nothing to improve the situation, and although Governor Hunter, who came to the colony in 1795, tried his best to stop the flood of spirits, he was not very successful. His successor, Governor King, was more determined. He published a number of orders aimed at prohibiting the import of spirits, in order to "put an end to the unwarranted and scandalous monopolies that have existed in this colony, and which has not only been the cause of much distress and ruin to the settlers and other institutions, but also of great injury to the public interest, and that of His Majesty's service."[14]

When in 1800 the *Follensby*, with James Parry of Newport, Rhode Island, as master, arrived with provisions and thirteen thousand gallons of spirits and seven thousand gallons of wine, and when at the same time the *Missouri*, under William Vickery of Philadelphia, arrived with seven thousand gallons of spirits and seven thousand gallons of wine, Governor King created a precedent. He bought the provisions but prohibited the landing of the spirits and wine. Captain Parry protested. His plea was "the assurance of those who had been here before that he could not fail of getting an unheard-of profit." Governor King remained unmoved.

[14] *Ibid.*, ser. 1, II:623.

To spare his colleagues a similar disappointment, Parry then asked the governor to send a letter to the American consul in London, informing him that American ships were no longer allowed to land spirits in Australia. This King did. He pointed out to the American consul that the import of spirits was forbidden and that the penalty for smuggling would be the confiscation of ship and cargo. He sent a similar letter to the British consul in America, telling him that no vessel would be allowed to land more than three hundred gallons of spirits.[15] This was the first diplomatic action concerning the relations between America and Australia.

In spite of threats and warnings, American ships continued to bring, and often succeeded in landing, spirits. King promulgated additional laws and orders. He took advantage of the presence of another American ship loaded with liquor to increase the duty and incidental landing charges and also to fix the sales price on these spirits, brought "for the purpose of impoverishing the Inhabitants, destroying their Health and subverting the Regularity necessary to be observed for the Prosperity of this Colony."[16]

But the perseverance of the American (and also the British) traders, the demand from the colonists for spirits, and the resistance of the profiteering officers proved too much for the governor. "I believe all the nations of the earth agreed to inundate the colony with spirits," he complained.[17] He became inconsistent in the application of his own orders. He failed to check the officers' monopoly and the traffic in spirits. Between September 1800 and October 1802 about seventy thousand gallons of spirits and thirty-three thousand gallons of wine, partly of American origin, were landed. The total population at that time was about thirty-five hundred.[18]

Although under King's orders large quantities of spirits and wines were sent away, the total imports increased constantly, and none of the succeeding governors was able to

[15] *Ibid.*, III:7, 56, 111, 413.
[16] *Ibid.*, v:85.
[17] Edward Shann, *An Economic History of Australia* (Cambridge, 1930), 37.
[18] *HRA*, ser. 1, III:p. xv.

halt the influx. How prominently spirits still figured in the economy of the colony in 1810 is shown by the fact that the governor got importers to finance the building of a much-needed hospital in exchange for a three-year monopoly for the import of forty-five thousand gallons of spirits. The traffic did not cease until the outbreak of the War of 1812.

Although the profits obtainable from the sale of spirits in New South Wales were certainly attractive to the American shipper, they were not his only motive. The risk of the dangerous reefs around the Australian coast, together with the discrimination by the colonial administration to which many American ships were subject, might have outweighed the attraction of possible profits. The shippers were interested in Australian trade mainly in connection with their China trade.

Almost every vessel calling at Port Jackson proceeded to China[19]—sometimes directly, sometimes after calling at the Fiji Islands or the Northwest Coast to take aboard a cargo for China. But finding a cargo for sale in China was no easy matter. Around 1800 China's foreign trade was a very one-sided affair. There were very few goods which the Chinese desired to purchase from westerners; sealskins, furs, sandalwood, and *béche-de-mer* were about the only commodities acceptable. So the western traders needed specie to pay for the many goods they wished to buy from China.

When the Americans entered the China trade, they had to compete with the powerful and well-established East India Company. Even for this company, backed by all the resources of a strong and well-developed England, it was difficult to find cargoes acceptable to Chinese merchants. Consequently, if the American trader wanted to break the firm grip of the East India Company and get a hold in the Chinese market, he had to make a favorable impression with hard cash. But cash was a rare commodity in the America of 1800, and here the New South Wales trade was very useful.

Of course, the young colony, too, had little cash. It was not supposed to have any. The British government had hoped

[19] See *ibid.*, IX:47.

that New South Wales might quickly become self-supporting and not need much specie.[20] All payments were made
either by barter or by drafts on London. The only persons to
have currency were the officers, until after 1800, when some
currency did get into the hands of the populace. The enormous purchase of American spirits quickly transferred what
specie there was in the colony into the hands of the Americans. With this specie and with drafts on London the Americans went to China to trade with the Hong merchants and to
destroy the monopoly of the East India Company. To judge
by available statistics, their efforts were quite successful.

The Chinese called a ship freighted with dollars a "rich
ship." "The reason why the Chinese favor the American trade
so much is on account of the great quantity of specie that is
brought there," said a witness during the parliamentary investigation of the affairs of the East India Company in 1830,
and another remarked, "If you pay in dollars, you can buy
upon far better terms." They all agreed that the Americans
had captured a considerable share of the profitable China
trade.[21]

No wonder, then, that the American merchants did not like
to miss the New South Wales business on their way to China.
If in addition they could pick up a cargo of sealskins along
the Northwest Coast or of sandalwood in the South Sea
Islands, their happiness was complete. "In choosing rout
around New Holland, two motives influence us," read the instructions to Captain Dexter of the *John Jay* in 1800, "1st, to
avoid Cruisers passing Streights of Sunda; 2nd, the advantage
of trade at New Holland, getting money or exchange for the
outward cargo."[22]

This aim of the American merchants was known to the

[20] Great Britain, House of Commons, *Journal*, xxxvi:311 (April 1, 1779).

[21] *Asiatic Journal*, n.s., iii:8 (September–December, 1830); cf. Timothy Pitkin, *A Statistical View of the Commerce of the United States of America* (New
York, 1817), 249.

[22] Quoted in William B. Weeden, "Early Oriental Commerce in Providence,"
Proceedings of the Massachusetts Historical Society, 3d ser., i:250 (1907–8).
The cruisers referred to were French.

colonial and home administrations. It was one more reason for discouraging American trade with the colony. The government in London instructed the governor of New South Wales to exert his best efforts "to prevent the current specie of the Colony from being carried out of it."[23] But the efflux of specie could not always be prevented. It was imperative to buy provisions from the Americans and at times even the liquor. A resident of the colony reported to the government in 1809: "So necessary, indeed, has it been found to admit the introduction of a certain quantity of Spirits . . . that when the supply . . . failed, Spirits have been purchased from American traders touching at the Colony, at the *serious sacrifice of every piece of coin it contained, money being the only payment which would be taken.*"[24] In London the Earl of Liverpool was quite aware that English ships reached New South Wales only very irregularly. He was also aware of Americans' practice of, as he expressed it, taking away dollars from the colony for the Chinese market. He hoped, though, that the more regular arrival of supplies from England would do away with the necessity of buying any American goods and that the trade of New South Wales "will henceforth be retained in its natural and proper channel."[25]

The hopes of the earl did not materialize until the Anglo-American war put an end to American-Australian trade. Arrivals of English ships remained irregular and comparatively rare. The reason for this, and for the consequent capture of a large part of Australia's foreign trade by the Americans, was the East India Company charter.

According to this charter, no ships were permitted to trade in that part of the globe in which Australia is situated without special permission of the company. This order, naturally, could be applied to British subjects only, and it was sufficient protection for the company's monopoly only as long as trade on the seven seas was mainly a British affair. When the Americans turned up and proved to be keen competitors in the Pacific trade, the effect of the charter changed.

[23] *HRA*, ser. 1, vii:479. [24] *Ibid.*, 202. [25] *Ibid.*, 479.

The East India Company was not itself interested in the comparatively small New South Wales trade, but it nonetheless insisted on its rights against potential British competitors, who were thus barred from commercial intercourse with the colony. Consequently, very few British merchants were able to send their ships to Port Jackson. They had to sit back and watch the Americans establishing a regular trade and making sizable profits. About seventy trading ships from America called during the period from 1792 to 1812, and in addition, from about 1800 on an ever-increasing number of American whalers dropped anchor in Australian waters.

This situation suited neither the British merchants nor the free inhabitants of New South Wales and their governor. They wanted freedom of trade. The London firm of Enderby and Company protested to the government in 1800: "The Americans, hearing that New South Wales is considered within the chartered Seas of the East India Company, and that no British Merchants can send Goods to that Colony without the Risque of Seizure, have at Times sent small Vessels there with Investments of Goods in their Way to India, or the North-West Coast of America, and have benefited themselves so much thereby, that there is no doubt if the restrictions are still continued against British Merchants sending Goods there, that they will Monopolize all the Advantages of the Trade to New South Wales, and this Country will have the Expense of supporting it."[26] A long petition, signed by one thousand citizens of the colony, asked the government to do away with the restrictions imposed by the charter of the East India Company.[27]

None of these protests produced any action on the part of the government. As a result, a large share of New South Wales trade was forced into illegal channels, or at least into the use of devious methods only in nominal accord with the law. It began with British merchantmen's trying to circumvent restrictions by hoisting American flags.[28] When this was prohibited or lost its effectiveness, British as well as Australian

[26] *HRA*, ser. 1, III:2; cf. *ibid.*, VII:501.   [27] *Ibid.*, x:55.   [28] *Ibid.*, v:16, 167.

merchants formed partnerships with American citizens—in order to justify their use of the American flag. The Americans, whose commerce was often discriminated against, could point to their British associations and trade more freely.[29]

Through this cooperation an entirely new trade was developed. Up to then the East India Company had shipped Chinese goods destined for Australia either to Bengal or even to London for transshipment. Since the American merchants were not interested in trading between China and New South Wales, no goods were flowing in that direction. The partnership of Australians with Americans made it possible to organize direct shipments from China to New South Wales. The costs of transshipping were eliminated, and the competition with the East India Company was increased.

London was opposed to the encroachment upon the East India Company's interests, and informed the governor of the colony accordingly. He tried to prevent the partnerships by prohibiting or making it difficult for settlers and Americans to get together. One of his orders, in 1804, prohibited Australians either from being hired by Americans or from going aboard their ships, and another forbade American ships to sail in Australian waters or to establish trading centers in New South Wales.[30] But it was easy to get around such orders. Something more drastic had to be done. The governor asked for instructions from London.

Before an answer reached him, however, two more Australian inhabitants applied for permission to establish a partnership with Americans. Their plan was to ship sandalwood and *bêche-de-mer* from the South Sea Islands to China and to bring back Chinese goods for the New South Wales market. This was legitimate trade and could only have been of benefit to the colony. But, bound by his instructions from London, Governor King had to refuse his permission for the partnership, although he himself would have liked to promote the commerce of the colony. When he wrote to his government about the application for the partnership, he stated: "As I

[29] *Ibid.*, v:16, 167, 119.   [30] *Ibid.*, 93. 167.

MIDWAY I.○

○ ○○○ HAWAIIAN
○ ISLANDS

○ WAKE I.

MARSHALL
ISLANDS

ISLANDS

FANNING I.○

○ CHRISTMAS I.

GILBERT ISLANDS

EQUATOR

.ELLICE
ISLANDS

SOLOMON
ISLANDS

NEW
HEBRIDES

FIJI ISLANDS

SAMOA
ISLANDS

SOCIETY
ISLANDS

NEW
CALEDONIA

AUSTRALIA
and the Islands of the Pacific

AUCKLAND

NEW
ZEALAND

conceive that Measure would lead to opening an Intercourse with this Colony and the Company's possessions, I have resisted the importunate Solicitations on that Behalf, as it militates so much against His Majesty's Instructions thereon; but in continuing those Restrictions I have assured the Adventuring Inhabitants, being His Majesty's Subjects, of my earnest wish and exertions to promote their Endeavours . . . and I cannot close this Subject without humbly suggesting the necessity of Instructions being sent prescribing the intercourse and connexion that may be allowed between the inhabitants and Americans."[31]

As a result of London's policy the two inhabitants did illegally what they were not permitted to do legally. Their procedure was characteristic of the methods used to overcome legal restrictions. They left on an English boat, ostensibly for London. When they had sailed for four days, they met the American ship at an appointed place and transferred to it. They then proceeded according to their original plan. When they returned from China aboard the American ship, the *Criterion* under Captain Peter Chace, they attempted to land their cargo of tea, silks, and nankins. They did not succeed. Thereupon they sailed to Hobart Town and renewed their attempt, again without success. The officials there had the same instructions as those in Port Jackson, and were determined to stop all commerce which ran counter to the interests of the East India Company.[32] Eventually the cargo was smuggled into the country. This clandestine commerce continued, in spite of the vigilance of the authorities, until the charter of the East India Company was revised and some of the restrictions upon Australian trade were eliminated.

The earliest relations between America and Australia, then, were purely commercial transactions, and many of them were outside the law. For this the British government's policy must largely be blamed. The attempt to prevent the Americans from trading with the new colony was anachronistic, and it indicated that the British government misjudged the char-

[31] *Ibid.*, 324.   [32] *Ibid.*, 719.

acter of the Yankee trader. It should have known that decrees, orders, and proclamations could not restrain the Boston and Philadelphia merchants in their quest for profits. The natural result of the government's action was to drive the relations between New South Wales and the United States into undesirable and illegitimate channels. A more progressive policy would no doubt have been more beneficial to all concerned. As it was, the advantage of trading was on the side of the Americans. They profited by the commerce with New South Wales, and, perhaps more important, this commerce helped them to break the monopoly of the East India Company in the Far East.

CHAPTER II

The Anglo-American War

THE Anglo-American war in 1812 provided statesmen and merchants in England with the means to destroy the unpopular American trade in the Pacific. The traders and shippers of New England and New York were furious at their President, whom they accused of having anti-commercial sympathies and of having provoked the war. "People of America!" began an article in the *Boston Columbian Centinel*. "Reflect on this conduct and sentiment. Cast your mind's eye back in the history of your beloved country and say, what would have been the condition of *North America*, had the commercial enterprise of your ancestors been destroyed by the Madisons of their day? Would it not have continued, like the southern and middle parts of this great continent, a nation of herdsmen and slavers? Yes."[1]

The people of the eastern seaboard had good reason to hate the war. The superior British fleet eventually undid the result of many decades of stubborn and adventurous pioneering by the young American merchant fleet. American trading ships all but disappeared from the seven seas, where they had just begun to be familiar sights.

Immediately upon the beginning of hostilities, the secretary of state in London sent a dispatch to Sydney ordering all the King's subjects to "do their utmost in their several Stations, to make Capture of the Ships and Vessels belonging to Citizens of the United States, and to destroy their Commerce."[2] The order was followed by detailed instructions to the governor for making exact returns as to captured American property and especially to dispose properly of the all important coin and bullion taken from the American ships.[3] This order was unfavorable to the colony. The economy of the set-

---

[1] January 6, 1813.   [2] *HRA*, ser. 1, VII:523.   [3] *Ibid.*, 557, 678, 685.

tlement was very shaky and dependent upon the importation of goods. Even in peacetime the arrival of English vessels had been irregular and at long intervals, and American supplies had been always a most welcome and often a vital supplement. Now the outbreak of war made the coming of English ships more doubtful yet, and eliminated American stores altogether. The colony had to rely on its own meager resources.

Other effects of the war upon the colony were less direct and severe. In November 1812 the American privateer *Holkar*, a ship with eighteen nine-pound guns and one hundred and thirty-seven men captured the British brig *Emu* on her way to Port Jackson. The *Emu's* crew of twenty-two men refused to fight—with the exception of two men—and her lieutenant was forced to sink the ship's papers and surrender to the Americans, who took the *Emu* to St. Vincent. The most precious part of the *Emu's* cargo were female convicts badly needed for settlement purposes in Tasmania. They never reached their destination, and their loss was much regretted.[4]

The spectacular exploits of Captain Porter with his frigate *Essex* aroused considerable interest and also affected Australia. The *Essex* was the first ship of the American navy to enter the Pacific, sent there mostly to protect whalers. The captain captured a large tonnage of British ships of all kinds, mainly whalers, before his ship was destroyed by the British frigate *Phoebe*. One of the victims of the *Essex* was the *Seringapatam*. She was brought, in September 1813, to the Marquesas, where Porter established a fortified base. During one of Porter's absences from the base, the British prisoners overpowered their American guards, sailed away on the *Seringapatam*, reached Port Jackson on July 1, 1814, and there reported on their adventures, revealing the disturbing news of the American base.[5]

One more event in which the colony and the Americans

[4] *HRA*, ser. 1, vii: 700, 728, 830; viii: 312, 352.

[5] *Ibid.*, 312, 350. David Porter, *Journal of a Cruise to the Pacific Ocean* (Philadelphia, 1815), and *A Voyage to the South Seas in the Years 1812–1814* (London, 1823).

were involved caused concern in London and Sydney. Early in the war the governor of the colony received a long report from England about a possible French attack with American help against Sydney. The source of the government's information was the Danish adventurer Jorgen Jorgensen, and the story of the plan was not any more reliable than Jorgensen himself. Nevertheless the British government took it seriously enough to warn the governor about the danger, requesting him to take all necessary precautions. In addition, the secretary of state, the Earl of Bathurst, sent to the Admiralty "Suggestions for defeating an attempt reported to be in preparation against New South Wales by a squadron of four French and one American Frigates."[6]

According to Jorgensen's report the motive of the French was the desire to acquire New South Wales as a base for fishing and whaling in the Pacific and for trading with South America and the East Indies. The American role in the enterprise was subordinate: two American fishermen, Kelly and Coleman, were to join the French with their ships, and lead them to Port Jackson. The Americans had been whaling along the colony's coast for some time, and knew the area well.[7] There seems to be no evidence in published American documents of any official support for these two men in the adventure, but in view of the general character of Americans to be found in the Pacific at that time the story is plausible.

Whether or not Jorgensen's report had any foundation in fact, the London government and the governor were disturbed by it, and their fear of an attack was not entirely unreasonable. Apprehension of a foreign attack upon the faraway and weak colony came into being almost with the first settlers. In February 1803 Secretary of State Lord Hobart, impressed by the many stories about possible foreign invasions, warned Governor King: "It is evident that the attention of other European powers has been drawn to that quarter of the

[6] HRA, ser. 1, VIII: 74ff, 653, 654.
[7] Ibid., 72, 654. For a detailed story of Jorgensen's report see Gordon Greenwood, Early American-Australian Relations (Melbourne, 1944), 105ff.

world, and it need scarcely be observed that the establishment of any foreign power on that part of the coast might, in the event of hostilities, greatly interrupt the communications with Port Jackson and materially endanger the tranquility and security of our possessions there."[8] Subsequent French and American activity in the Pacific increased British suspicions both at home and in the colony.

France had shown an early and persistent interest in New South Wales and the South Seas. Maupertuis and de Brosses had written about them. Bougainville, Dufresne, and La Pérouse had sailed there. The scientific expedition of Baudin in 1802 with the ships *Géographe* and *Naturaliste* stirred up a rumor that the real purpose of the expedition was to find a place for settlement in Van Diemen's Land, or to settle on the northwest coast of Bass Strait. Taking no chances, Governor King at that time asked for and received permission to anticipate any French surprises by occupying Tasmania and founding Port Phillip and Hobart.[9] Péron, the historian of the Baudin expedition, dwelt at some length upon the military weakness of Sydney, and even advised General Decaen, governor of Mauritius to "destroy it as soon as possible." Baudin himself suggested that the French should quickly restore the balance in the South Seas, which was disturbed by the rapid development of the British possession there. Finally, in 1810, presumably basing his order upon Baudin's reports, Napoleon directed Decaen to replenish his depleted supplies by a conquest of Port Jackson. But the battle of Trafalgar had, five years earlier, assured the security of Australia from French attacks, and Napoleon's defeat in 1814 removed the threat of French conquest forever.[10]

Fear of American attacks was less specific but almost equally strong. The entrance of the American Navy into the Pacific and the activity of American privateers against British ship-

[8] *Historical Records of New South Wales* (Sydney, 1893–1901), v:833.

[9] *Ibid.*, IV:766; *HRA*, ser. 1, IV:249; *Cambridge History of the British Empire*, VII, pt. 1, 80ff.

[10] *Ibid.*, 83, 97; *ibid.*, II, "The New Empire, 1783–1870," 122; Ernest Scott, *Terre Napoleon* (London, 1910).

ping with "mortifying results" were in themselves a disturbing development and long remembered.[11] The establishment of American bases on the Marquesas, Sandwich, and Society islands threatened to make this new American influence in the Pacific permanent. All the presumed or real dangers implied in French and American activities caused anxiety in the minds of English and colonial statesmen which never quite disappeared, and which influenced their policy for a long time to come.

Although the war had temporarily halted American trade with Australia, fear that it might be resumed continued to haunt the minds of British statesmen. During the great debate over the renewal of the East India Company's charter in 1813 the success of American merchants in the company's exclusive zones was constantly cited as a point against continuing the monopoly. In a petition the merchants of Liverpool, Glasgow, Bristol, and other cities, fighting for the right to trade in the hitherto exclusive areas of the East India Company, based much of their argument on the company's failure to exploit its monopoly and the consequent advantage thus accruing to the Americans. This situation was described at the time as the whole issue between the company and the commercial and manufacturing part of the British public.[12] It was strange, one member of Parliament complained, that "what British merchants were deprived of should be given to the Americans."[13]

Another speaker wondered in connection with the company's claim that only a monopoly in China could be satisfactory, why it was that other nations, particularly the Ameri-

---

[11] *London Courier*, June 2, 1813; *HRA*, ser. 1, IX:57, 849; George Coggeshall, *History of the American Privateers* (New York, 1856), 316; *Niles' Register*, IV:125 (1813).

[12] See "Papers respecting the Negociation for a Renewal of the East India Company's exclusive Privileges, 1812," *Quarterly Review*, VIII:249ff (1812); "Report of the Committee of Correspondence of the East India Company," *Pamphleteer*, II:94ff (1813); F. W. Howay, ed., *Voyages of the "Columbia" to the Northwest Coast* (Massachusetts Historical Society, 1941), p. xxvff; *Revue Britannique*, I:140ff (1825); *Salem Gazette*, June 24, 1828.

[13] *London Courier*, June 2, 1813.

cans, had been able to carry on such a lucrative trade with China. "What virtue there might be in the American character that was not in the British, it remained for the Advocates of monopoly to shew: for his own part he knew of none that could make the intercourse with China more dangerous in the persons of British subjects than of Americans."[14] And yet another speaker referred to the "immense source of opulence to American merchants which the circuitous trade to India enjoyed by America had offered," having in mind the sailings of American traders from one Pacific country to another, all within the company's exclusive jurisdiction. Trade connections created by Americans were used as well by Englishmen, Australians, and others in order to evade the company's monopoly. This was true of routes between Australia and China, already mentioned, and also between Australia and India, China and India, and eventually Europe and India.[15]

The antimonopoly argument was convincing. At the debate's end a bill was passed removing New South Wales from the company's jurisdiction. This change, combined with the Navigation Acts, allowed British shipping to ply directly between England and the colony, satisfying the demands of many settlers.[16] At the end of the war with America, therefore, the London government expressed in a dispatch to Sydney the hope that traffic between England and New South Wales could be resumed by English ships en route to China. The governor was reminded that trade of foreign vessels with the colony was directly at variance with the Navigation Acts. Such trade had formerly been tolerated on the plea of neces-

[14] *London Times,* July 2, 1813.

[15] *London Courier,* June 2, 1813; Holden Furber, "The Beginning of American Trade with India, 1784–1812," *New England Quarterly,* xi:235 (1938); "Memoir of Elias Hasket Derby, Merchant of Salem, Massachusetts," *Hunt's Merchant Magazine,* xxxvi:173 (1857); "Report of the Committee of Correspondence," 118.

[16] There still was a limitation upon the size of vessels permitted to sail to New South Wales which was not lifted until 1819. Only ships of more than 350 tons were permitted. This eliminated much trade since it was uneconomical to send such big ships. See *HRA,* ser. 1, x:196, 809.

sity, but now, in view of the cancellation of the East India Company's monopoly, more regular shipping could be expected, and foreign ships should be admitted only for repair, not for trade.[17]

This obvious reference to America did not altogether please the Australian colonists, who favored trade with the Yankees although they feared the Americans as a threat to their security. This fear persisted long after the war, and in 1827 the *Sydney Gazette* summed up Australia's attitude. It recounted the various activities of France and America which clearly aimed at the extension of influence in the Pacific. American communications with many islands and native kings were disliked as a threat to Australia's security. Great Britain should extend its dominion in the Pacific. The *Gazette* suspected that America was jealous of the growing British influence and bent upon "annoying" the colony "at no distant day." Americans should also keep away from the "innumerable isles that bespeck that ocean of which Australia is destined to hold the imperial sway." No foreign power should gain influence among the islands in the immediate neighborhood of an empire like Australia to which Great Britain gave birth.[18]

There were dissenting voices in the minority. The *Australian* believed that the population of the colony was too small and poor to indulge in the ambitious project of controlling the whole continent. They suggested instead concentration upon New South Wales and an invitation to the French or some other foreign nation to settle on the faraway shores of Australia. Then "beneficial intercourse would naturally spring up. Our jealousy of any foreign power resembles the very mistaken policy against alien immigrants holding land." Enlightened states, the article concluded, encourage foreigners who are carriers of the arts and knowledge of their lands.[19]

The fear of the settlers and the resulting desire for greater

[17] *HRA*, ser. 1, VIII:648.

[18] *Sydney Gazette*, August 24, 1827.

[19] *Asiatic Journal*, VII:97 (February 1832); see Jean Ingram Brookes, *International Rivalry in the Pacific Islands, 1800–1875* (Berkeley, 1941), 7.

help from the motherland and exclusive control over the chain of islands stretching around Australia became permanent elements in Australian policy. It is remarkable indeed how little change has taken place. The *Gazette* statement of this policy has been repeated at regular intervals with little variation. Today Australia is still the foremost exponent of closer empire cooperation and improved imperial defense among the Dominions, and the Australian–New Zealand agreement of January 1944 indicated that Australia will not renounce regional arrangements even under a world security organization.

Notwithstanding these fears, and in spite of London's admonition to the governor not to trade with foreigners, American trade with the colony was resumed after the war. Supplies from England were slow in coming. So when the first American schooner, the *Traveller*, arrived from China at Port Jackson, Governor Macquarie was happy about the restoration of American commercial contacts with the colony. "Pleased with the Prospect of a beneficial Intercourse being thus renewed by this first Arrival of an American since the Treaty of Peace," he granted permission for the merchandise to be landed in the spring of 1816.

His pleasure was soon marred, however, by the rather unholy character of one of his army chaplains. During the governor's absence in the interior of the country, the Reverend Benjamin Vale seized the ship as a lawful prize under the Navigation Acts. Upon learning of this act, the governor immediately removed the arrest and restraint, "conceiving that there was no Law prohibiting such Trade, and knowing that the Constant Usage and Custom of this Place, from its first becoming A British Settlement, has been Invariably (in Times of Peace) to Admit American Ships and Cargoes to come to Entry in every Respect as if they Were British Property." The *Traveller*, he pointed out, was the forty-second ship to come to Port Jackson under American colors, and nobody, neither his predecessors nor his legal adviser, had ever objected. Although he did not want to make need an excuse if the action was illegal, he also wanted to remind the government in London that the acquisition of the tea, sugar, and other merchandise from the Americans was a necessity, as they were otherwise unobtainable.

The London government recognized the governor's plea of not guilty on the grounds of a precedent of twenty-five years' trade with Americans. For the future, however, it insisted upon strict adherence to the Navigation Acts. London believed that the colony had now reached a stage where foreign trade could be dispensed with. The colony was thus forbidden to accept American merchandise except in cases of need, when the rules might be relaxed.[20] This new enforcement of the Navigation Acts was effective, and reduced American-Australian trade to almost nothing. At intervals of several years an American ship would call at an Australian port, or occasionally American goods would reach the colony via China, but there was no regularity in these dealings.[21]

[20] *HRA*, ser. 1, IX:42ff.   [21] *Ibid.*, 109.

CHAPTER III

Whaling and Sealing

THE suppression of regular trade between America and New South Wales did not interrupt relations between the two countries altogether, except during the war years. The number of American whalers and sealers in the Pacific was so large that during the first half century more fishing vessels called on ports in New South Wales and other Australian colonies than all American trading ships together.

Australian whaling had begun in 1791, when some English ships on their way to New South Wales noticed whales and decided to investigate whaling possibilities before proceeding to the American coast for fishing. The reports of the captains were favorable and were confirmed by subsequent investigations. But the unfavorable weather of the New South Wales coast drove the whalers away to the more familiar grounds.

The governors of the colony were more persistent. The establishment of a whaling industry would be most beneficial to the young economy, and from the very first the colonial officials lent their full support to the development of whaling, and advertised the quality of Australian waters.[1] Governor Phillip sent optimistic reports to London, but complained that none of the whalers would give the coast a fair trial. The more attractive fur trade along the American Northwest Coast and trade among the South Sea Islands, he suspected, were the real reason for the fishermen's departure—not the bad weather and the currents around the colony's coast. Secretary of State Dundas agreed with the governor about the prospects of whaling, which would "eventually become an object of great consequence to the settlement, and be a means

[1] *HRA*, ser. 1, I:303, 307, 312, 348, 397; William John Dakin, *Whalemen Adventurers* (Sydney, 1934), 8. For a brief history of Australian whaling, see Lindsay G. Thompson, *History of the Fisheries of New South Wales* (Sydney, 1893), chap. VII.

of extending the communication betwixt it and this country
(as well as others) much beyond that necessary degree there-
of which attains at present."[2]

Subsequent governors continued Phillip's pioneering work,
and went to considerable length in the sponsorship of Australian whaling.[3] Their efforts, together with the Spanish difficulties and wars which made South American waters unsafe,
eventually shifted the interest of whalemen from the eastern
to the southern and southwest Pacific. But the governors
must soon have felt like the master of the sorcerer's appren-
tice, for thanks to the restrictive laws of Great Britain the
colonists gained little profit from the whaling, and the Americans caused unending trouble. American whalers came early.
The secret of rich rewards in Australian waters could not be
kept from them for very long. The *General Boyd* sailed into
Sydney in June 1802, reportedly the first American whaler,
and others followed in rapid succession.

American whalemen did not represent the human race at
its best. A hiring agent told applicants, "A whaler, gentlemen, is a place of refuge for the distressed and persecuted, a
school for the dissipated, an asylum for the needy. There is
nothing like it. You can see the world."[4] The crews were
mixed, to say the least, and the long, dangerous voyages
tended to bring out their worst characteristics. Nor did the
nature of the Australian colonies and their settlers help matters any. "There are few places which surpass these localities
for the commission of all kinds of vice; and in saying this, I
have reference as well to those of South and West Australia,
as to those of New Zealand . . ." wrote Captain Wilkes,
chief of the American Pacific exploring expedition.[5] And some
American missionaries to Australia in their first report to
Boston remarked, ". . . the mass of the population presents
the most unfavorable aspect." The missionaries, however,

---

[2] *HRA*, ser. 1, I:312, 348, 354.

[3] *Ibid.*, I:397; II:369; III:438, 514ff.

[4] Quoted by Dakin, *Whalemen Adventurers*, 63.

[5] Charles Wilkes, *Narrative of the United States Exploring Expedition* (Philadelphia, 1845), v:494.

were somewhat consoled because at least "great outward respect" was paid to the Lord's Day.[6]

Many American whalemen proved to be extreme nuisances to the colonial government. They would hire colonists as crew members or to form rather rough fishing gangs, then drop them on some faraway island when they were no longer needed.[7] Frequently convicts were able to escape on American ships. In one case a whaler was specially prepared in the United States for assisting in the escape of some Irish Fenians from Western Australia. The whaler prevented police action by showing the American flag. A diplomatic incident was avoided only because the British government thought the case unsuitable for diplomatic action.[8]

Rowdyism increased when American sealers arrived and began to fight with colonial sealers for the best grounds. Complaints came in large numbers from colonial seamen about the rough treatment they received at the hands of the Americans, but natives on the many islands and in the undeveloped areas of the colonies fared even worse than the colonists.[9] The bad behavior of the Americans absorbed much of the governors' time and was a perennial subject of their correspondence with London. But, after all, these problems were not different in kind from those which a large group of the colony's population presented. It was the inroads Americans made upon the whaling and sealing trade in Australian waters that concerned the governors most.

Keen competition was expected, and attempts were made to curb it. Even before the arrival of American whalers Governor King inquired in London how they should be treated, and implied in his inquiry the desire that he might be permitted to prohibit their activity.[10] After the Americans had

[6] *Missionary Herald*, xxi:388 (1825).   [7] *HRA*, ser. 1, v:167, 656.

[8] J. S. Battye, *Western Australia* (Oxford, 1924), 332ff; M. Masson and J. F. Jameson, "The Odyssey of Thomas Muir," *American Historical Review*, xxix: 49ff (1923); *HRA*, ser. 1, ii:235.

[9] *HRA*, ser. 1, v:814; Dakin, *Whalemen Adventurers*, 22; James Morton Callahan, *American Relations in the Pacific and Far East, 1784–1900* (Baltimore, 1901), 37ff.

[10] *HRA*, ser. 1, iii:636, 642.

arrived, King recommended to London that the introduction of American vessels into Australian waters should be checked, lest "any benefit this Colony may possess would become the property of Americans at the Expense of England."[11] His fearful anticipation soon became a reality. American aggressiveness, colonial apathy, and the selfishness of the East India Company combined to further the success of American whaling in the west Pacific.

A number of urgent petitions from the colonial governors and the English merchants resulted in government permission for whalers to sail from England to Australia. This concession by the East India Company was extended to permit whalers to carry goods instead of ballast on their outward voyage, so that the Americans would not "monopolize all the advantages of the trade to New South Wales."[12] But the liberality of the company, while stimulating colonial fisheries somewhat, was not sufficient. As long as colonists were forbidden to send their products to England, their whaling enterprise could not really be successful. The pleas of Governor King for permission to build ships in the colony and take fishery produce in these ships to England and even to China came to naught.[13] The company was not willing to surrender this privilege until forced to do so, in part at least, in 1813.

When the governors failed in their attempts to lift the legal restrictions upon a free development of colonial whaling enterprise, the only means left for stopping a trend that seemed disadvantageous to the colony's welfare was to hamper American whalers within territorial Australian waters. This promised some success, since American ships conveniently used the colony for repairs and provisions and were absolutely dependent upon a land base when bay whaling developed.

So within the narrow limits of their jurisdiction the governors promulgated various orders, between 1800 and 1812,

[11] Ibid., v: 602.

[12] Ibid., iii: 765; Dakin, Whalemen Adventurers, 7ff.

[13] HRA, ser. 1, v: 203; John Thomas Bigge, Report of the Commissioner of Inquiry, on the State of Agriculture and Trade in the Colony of New South Wales (London, 1823), 56.

designed to counteract American activity in New South Wales and its dependencies. Governmental restrictions upon the domicile of foreigners in the colony were an attempt to prevent Americans from establishing a fishing industry. A law that sealing and whaling vessels could be cleared from a colonial port only to another port, but not to return to the same port, was intended to keep the Americans on the move. The American practice of building ships on the Australian coast "in violation of international and local laws" was to be stopped by prohibiting the building of vessels exceeding fourteen feet. British seamen were forbidden to accept employment with American sealers and whalers.[14]

All these rules could not be effectively enforced. The area in which the Americans pursued their trade was enormous and undeveloped, and the colonial government did not have sufficient means of enforcement. Besides, mere inconveniences and legal pin-pricking could not frighten the Americans away from their profitable business. American whalemen were little troubled by the law.

Neither the efforts of the colonial governors nor the Anglo-American war stopped American whaling and sealing in and near Australian waters. On the contrary, American enterprise quickly developed into considerable proportions, soon outranking colonial and British whaling and sealing fisheries. (Colonial sealing assumed larger proportions than whaling.) Reasons for the inferiority of colonial whaling were not too difficult to find: The colonists lacked capital and those with some funds were more attracted to sheep breeding; even the liberalized charter of the East India Company still handicapped the colonists; and British fishing interests feared competition from the colony, whose whaling, if ever permitted to develop freely, would have many advantages over fishing fleets from far away.[15]

To explain the inferiority of British whaling to American whaling is more difficult. The discrepancy was striking. In 1845 about seven hundred vessels manned by twenty thou-

[14] *HRA*, ser. 1, v:93, 203.   [15] *Australian Handbook* (Sydney, 1889), 143.

sand men were engaged in American whaling. In 1841 England had only eighty-five ships and three thousand men, while in 1821 it had had three hundred and twenty ships with thirteen thousand men. English whaling decreased while American whaling soared. In the middle of the century, when Anglo-American relations were not too friendly, this condition gave concern to Englishmen, not for economic reasons but because of problems of maritime power. Whalemen made good navy men.[16]

A letter to the *London Times* by an expert summed up the reasons for the decline of British whaling: "The greater cost of fitting out whalers here,[17] the drunkenness, incapacity and want of energy of the masters and crews. I have known English whalers to be out four years and take 1,300 or 1,400 barrels of oil; and American vessels cruising almost on the same 'ground' would probably have captured twice as much." The discipline on board American ships was highly praised, then: "I have little sympathy for Americans; for as a body I do not believe you could well find a more dishonest people; but their energy in bringing this trade to the pitch it has arrived at deserves the highest encomium."[18]

At the peak of whaling the majority of American vessels were in the Pacific. They could be found near the South Sea Islands, Tasmania, New Zealand, and Australia. Bay whaling forced them to establish shore stations, and as a result Americans came in close contact with the land and the population. The main meeting place on the Australian continent was Western Australia. Americans were there earlier and in greater numbers and knew more about the territory than the British. "It is due to the Americans to state that we are more

[16] *London Times*, June 9, 1846; "The Australian Colonies," *Quarterly Review*, LXVIII:143 (1841).

[17] A ship costing £8200 to build in England was estimated to cost only £5000 in the United States; cf. E. Keble Chatterton, *Whalers and Whaling* (London, 1924), 154.

[18] *London Times*, June 18, 1846. The firm of Enderby, which had inaugurated whaling in Australia, attempted to revive British whaling there with much fanfare and considerable expense, but did not succeed; cf. Chatterton, *Whalers and Whaling*, chap. XIV.

indebted to them than to any others for our knowledge of the inlets and anchorages of the Western seabord," wrote Nathaniel Ogle in 1838.[19] Indeed, the Americans were partly responsible for the colonization of Western Australia.

Fear of French plans for a settlement somewhere on the south or west coast of Australia led to the establishment of a British settlement in King George's Sound in 1826.[20] When the expedition on arrival at the Sound reported to the governor the presence of a large number of American sealers and whalers, fear of possible American plans was added to fear of the French.[21] After a few months the King George's Sound settlement proved unsatisfactory, and its founder, Captain Stirling, urged the immediate seizure of land near the Swan River. He ended his letter, "Finally, Sir, at a time when we have one French Vessel of War in these Seas with objects not clearly understood, and when we hear of an American Vessel of War being also in this neighbourhood, seeking a place for a Settlement, it becomes important to prevent them from occupying a position of such Value, particularly as you were pleased to say that His Majesty's Government is desirous of not being anticipated in such views by any Foreign Power."[22]

Stirling was permitted to investigate conditions in the Swan River area, and his favorable report was forwarded to London. The Admiralty, asked for an opinion, was not enthusiastic, and stated that "No other motive . . . than the political one of preventing other nations, as the French or Americans, of possessing themselves of the south-west corner of New Holland, should induce us to anticipate them; and even in the event of its falling into the hands of the one or the other of these powers, it would be a long series of years before they could give our other colonies much annoyance."[23]

The settlement project was abandoned, mainly for reasons

[19] *The Colony of Western Australia* (London, 1839).

[20] Battye, *Western Australia,* chap. III.

[21] Cf. Edmund Fanning, *Voyages and Discoveries in the South Seas, 1792–1832* (Salem, 1924), 232, 243.

[22] *HRA,* ser. 1, XII : 775ff.

[23] Battye, *Western Australia,* 67.

of economy, but Captain Stirling continued to agitate for it. A change in the London government brought a friend of Stirling's into high position, and the scheme was reconsidered. The Admiralty reversed its former position, and was suddenly quite concerned about an early establishment of the settlement. ". . . the sooner the better," the Admiralty said this time, "as the publication of the chart containing so fine an anchorage, entirely overlooked by the French navigators, may induce that nation, or the Americans, who are prowling about for some detached settlement, to assume possession of the only spot on the western coast of New Holland that is at all inviting for such purpose, to which we could have no right to offer any resistance."[24] On May 2, 1829, Great Britain took formal possession of the west coast of Australia.

There was no scheme afoot in the United States (or in France) to take possession of any part of the Australian continent. American warships were in the vicinity to protect American vessels and to maintain order among them.[25] Nevertheless, the presence of many American whalers and sealers along the coast was reason enough for the government's anxiety. A number of the Americans were more than transients; they had settled in various parts of west and southwest Australia for several reasons. Some had been shipwrecked; some came to do business; some had deserted their ships because of bad catches.[26]

Altogether, Americans were of considerable importance in the development of Western Australia. They had begun to play their role in presettlement days, and continued to play it after 1829. The trade they brought helped to overcome the initial hardships of the slowly growing colony.[27] Once the existence of the colony was assured, this trade grew into larger proportions. In 1840 and 1841, for instance, eight or

[24] *Ibid.*, 69ff.

[25] See *The Patriot* (Concord, N. H.), May 30, 1836; Wilkes, *Narrative*, v: 500.

[26] Dakin, *Whalemen Adventurers*, 61; George Granville Putnam, *Salem Vessels and their Voyages* (Salem, 1930), 43, 58; L. G. Churchward, "Australian-American Relations during the Gold Rush," *Historical Studies, Australia and New Zealand*, ii: footnote 13 (April 1942).

[27] Thomas Dunbabin, *The Making of Australasia* (London, 1922), 137.

more ships a month arrived at the Swan River.[28] Usually they remained there for some time, selling American goods, bartering, or taking on stores.[29] English vessels, on the other hand, appeared in very small numbers. This "apathy of the English in neglecting such an important trade is deservedly reprobated," said a report from the colony.[30]

In absolute figures the trade between the United States and all the colonies on the Australian continent was not important. The colonial economy was too much hemmed in by artificial obstacles. The privileges of the East India Company made any trade extremely difficult, and the British government together with merchant interests in London discouraged independent trade from the colonies, making trade even with the mother country practically impossible by imposing high British duties.[31] Under these circumstances there were few possibilities left for colonial exporters.

At one time Sydney merchants had tried their luck in a devious inter-island and China trade, but failed because of American competition. Their shipments of South Sea products to China in return for tea had to cease, they complained, because "of interference in this branch of trade by certain foreigners, who, through an American interest at Canton and the Isle of France, have been able to procure facilities for their trade, as well as protection for the vessel in which it is carried on."[32]

Exports from New South Wales to the United States were sporadic and practically nonexistent. Wool was the colony's only staple for export, and occasionally some quantities of it were shipped to America,[33] but here too regular trade was

[28] Battye, *Western Australia*, 471; *Asiatic Journal*, xxxii:331 (August 1840), xxxvii:334 (April 1842).

[29] Putnam, *Salem Vessels*, 60.

[30] *Asiatic Journal*, xxxii:331 (August 1840).

[31] Landed proprietors in the colony demanded that their products should be admitted into Great Britain at reduced rates, especially tobacco, which if encouraged "would soon rival that of Virginia." *Asiatic Journal*, ii:27 (May 1830).

[32] Bigge, *Report of the Commissioner of Inquiry*, 57, 60; Peter M. Cunningham, *Two Years in New South Wales* (London, 1827), ii:67.

[33] *Asiatic Journal*, xxxiii:30 (September 1840).

prevented by artificial barriers. The clerk of the American ship *Grotius* pondered much on the tariff question while he was in Australian waters, and he finally wrote out his ideas as to its effect on developments in America.

Incidentally we have noticed the opposition of the United States tariff in regard to Australian wool, as the writer viewed the subject, and its effect upon our manufacturing, mercantile and, to some extent also, our agricultural and producing interests. Let us say further, that this Island Continent, Australia, and adjacent colonies ever have been willing and in their earlier days anxious to sell or barter their only great staple product, wool, the finest in the world, for all of the above.

These shipments of ours to Australia were profitable enough usually to defray the expenses of a voyage. But whence would come a direct remittance freight of cargo home to remunerate the owner for his trouble? His ship must either look for a great additional expense, delay attending an uncertain trade, toward India, waiting months perhaps for company through the Torres Straits, or by the other route to China. Besides, how could conveniently the ordinary merchant, so long out of remittance, meet notes payable for outward shipments, or if venturing investment in wool, at arrival pay the heavy customs duties, unable as then he was to bond in warehouse and sell at option. Thus clogs of all kinds were imposed on the United States in this Australian trade. Thus poor and rich have been compelled to pay 30 or 40 per cent indirect taxation on all imported fine wool clothing, and the United States statistics long have shown the unnecessary, immense revenue therefrom.

Investigation will show, of this trite and complicated subject, how incalculable has been the loss of wages for these long years, by this tariff prohibition of Australian wool, to American workmen! For they are, or in a little while can become, as capable of manufacturing finest broadcloths as the English, only give them the proper material instead of masses of shoddy and coarse wool mixed with little of the obliged-to-be-imported fine wool; and which is placed on the market as finest American cloths. Who, moreover, can tell the benefit that might have thus resulted to the United States from an expert competition in this business.

It is well known at Salem that, many years ago, mills at either Andover or Framingham, Mass., were in contemplation of erection for manufacture of large cargoes of this Australian wool. But this enterprise was prevented by a succession of high tariff men, lobbyists, etc., all for a few special interests. The American grower would have received ample, reasonable protection for his sorts of wool. But we see that American people, poor or rich, will have the best if they can get it, home or imported.

If one would consider, too, the loss of our markets in Australia by these United States prohibitory tariffs for American surplus manufactures, together with the incidental loss of wages consequent thereon to American workmen, let him examine one of these invoices for the past fifty years. There will be found an assortment too tedious to specify—carriages, wagons, iron machinery and wares, furniture, all articles of domestic use, etc., of produce, butter, cheese, lard, hams, pork, fish, pickles, syrups, nuts, dried fruits, biscuit, flour, hops, etc..

The same principle holds here in its effects as regards generally this prohibition from abroad on materials for shipbuilding, and seamen's incidental wages lost to them thereby. What merchant or sailor does not know that for these long years, too, the cost of a three or four-hundred-ton ship has been five or ten thousand dollars more, at least, and so on of larger ones proportionally? The ruinous effects of United States tariffs on our Australian trade as relevant only has been commented upon, although it is lamentable to believe that they are the same in many others.[34]

In spite of the limited trade between America and the Australian colonies, a consul, James H. Williams, was appointed for Sydney in May 1836. He received a very friendly welcome from the colonial community. His presence was regarded "as a pledge of increasing intimacy between the two countries, from which mutual advantages may be expected to flow." In typical fashion the newspapers pondered over the similarities between the colony and the United States, and found consolation in the fact that America also had once started as a dependent territory. In 1843 a consul was appointed for Hobart and in 1852 for Melbourne.[35] These ap-

[34] Putnam, *Salem Vessels*, 62ff.

[35] Department of State Consular Dispatches, Sydney, I, August 22, 1836 (hereafter cited as Dispatches, Sydney); Melbourne, I, May 17, 1853; New South Wales, *Government Gazette*, February 6, 1839; *Sydney Morning Herald*,

pointments were an indication of the growing interest of the United States in the Australian continent, and the dispatch of the exploratory expedition under Charles Wilkes in 1839 showed that this interest extended to the whole Pacific. As the petitioners for this expedition expressed it, the intercourse of Americans with islands and countries of the Pacific had "become a matter of public interest, and deserving the protective care of the National Legislature."[36]

January 12, 1837; *The Colonist,* January 19, 1837; *The Australian,* January 17, 1859; A. R. Hasse, *Index to United States Documents Relating to Foreign Affairs* (Washington, 1921), III:1707, 1710, 1712.

[36] *House Document No. 179,* 20th Cong., 1st Sess., 1828. The arrival of the Wilkes expedition, like that of many subsequent ones, was the occasion of many festivities in Sydney. *Sydney Gazette,* December 3, 28, 1839; *The Australian,* December 14, 1839.

CHAPTER IV

The Gold Rushes

AMERICAN-AUSTRALIAN relations became very lively and intense when gold was discovered in California. The first news of the discoveries, reaching Australia toward the end of 1848, was received with considerable skepticism, but upon confirmation of the news, Australians too were seized by the "yellow fever." Emigration to the American West Coast began. The press of mercantile Sydney was happy at the prospects of new trade relations, but Melbourne suffered from a labor shortage and tried to discourage the exodus of badly needed men. Eight ships filled with gold-seekers left Sydney in January 1849, and in June some emigrants sailed from Melbourne.[1]

After this first batch of ships had left Sydney, emigration was halted until news of the fate of the first emigrants could reach Australia. Between April and June 1849 the arrival of only forty-three male and three female immigrants was reported from California.[2] Australians were still skeptical. But the arrival of a ship from San Francisco with twelve hundred ounces of gold on board convinced the most incredulous. A wave of emigration set in. Even men who had just been sent to the colonies from Great Britain with the assistance of public funds joined in the departures without staying long enough to do one day's work.

By December 1849 about eight hundred Australians and Tasmanians had reached California.[3] During the early months of 1850 the number of emigrants increased many fold, but

[1] Churchward, "Australian-American Relations," 14ff.

[2] *New York Herald,* August 13, 1849.

[3] Mary Floyd Williams, *History of the San Francisco Committee of Vigilance of 1851* (Berkeley, 1921), 123; Edward H. Hargraves, *Australia and its Gold Fields* (London, 1855), 72, 119; cf. *New York Herald,* May 30, June 24, December 8, 1849, February 7, 1850.

toward the end of that year it slowed down, and during the first half of 1851 more persons returned to Australia than left. The discovery of gold in Australia occasioned this reversal. The disposition for emigrating to California quickly abated and parties who had engaged passage forfeited their passage money, "being convinced that they were going to a distance to seek that which was to be found at the door," said a contemporary report.[4] However, before Australians returned home they helped to populate and develop California.

This British element in the development of California was welcomed in England. "It is impossible," wrote the *London Times,* "but that British and Anglo-American influence should pervade that great ocean and soften the inveterate jealousy of China and Japan." Also, the route to Australia and New Zealand would be shortened, and the many ships already in California were proof that the two settlements would trade with other countries in the Pacific.[5]

But the Californians were not ready to look so far ahead. They had to grapple with more immediate problems, caused largely by the Australians. Some of the Australian emigrants were escaped convicts, ex-convicts, or convicts on parole who were free to go anywhere except Great Britain. They soon banded themselves together in San Francisco, Sacramento, and other centers, constituting a large percentage of the criminal elements abounding in these cities. Their criminal fraternities dated back in many instances to mutual acquaintance in Sydney or on board ship.[6] They were not strictly organized in gangs, but as soon as they began functioning they helped and supported each other, thus creating the impression of a well-established group of gangsters hard to break up. Ignorance of the exact nature or size of the Australian gangs magnified their danger in the eyes of the Californian population, and almost every Australian was soon under

[4] *New York Herald,* May 13, 1850.

[5] May 4, 1850.

[6] Mary Floyd Williams, *Papers of the San Francisco Committee of Vigilance of 1851* (Berkeley, 1919), 30, 69ff, 77, *et al.; Illustrated London News,* XXIII: 71 (1853).

suspicion and liable to be lynched at the slightest provoca-
tion. "Sydney Town," in northeast San Francisco, was the
residential district of most Australians, and the "Sydney
Ducks" or "Sydney Coves" were held responsible—in many
cases without justification—for most of the murders, rob-
beries, and fires occurring in the city.[7]

The illegal activities of these Australian immigrants contributed much to the success of antiforeign agitation in California and to the desire for the restriction of immigration.[8]
A bill introduced into the California legislature "for the
Better Regulation of the Mines and the Government of
Foreign Miners" was designed mainly to restrict the activities
of foreigners. The legislative committee on finance, in its report supporting the bill, advocated a tax on foreign diggers,
referring to the huge immigration to be expected and the
many immigrants already present who represented only "the
commencement of a vast multitude *en route* and preparing
to come hither, of the worst population of the Mexican and
South American States, New South Wales," and other areas.
The committee resented "the convicts of Mexico, Chihli and
Botany Bay" turned out by the boatload daily upon the
shores of California and "carrying away immense treasures."[9]
Another bill, making it a felony to bring convicts into the
state, was also passed, but it was never effectively enforced.[10]

Eventually the crimes of Australians and other groups,
especially in San Francisco, gave rise to the Committee of
Vigilance in 1851. This committee assigned to itself the task
of preventing crime and apprehending and punishing criminals. John Jenkins, a notorious criminal from Sydney, was
the first prisoner of the committee and the first to be hanged.[11]
Others followed in large numbers. The prophylactic activity

[7] Williams, *History*, 170, 239, *et al.*; Frank Soulé *et al.*, *The Annals of San Francisco* (New York, 1855), 223, 257; Alonzo Delano, *Across the Plains and among the Diggings* (New York, 1936), 158, 159.

[8] Williams, *History*, 126.

[9] *New York Herald*, May 13, 1850.

[10] Williams, *History*, 122.

[11] Williams, *Papers*, 14ff; Georgia Willis Read and Ruth Gaines, eds., *Gold Rush* (New York, 1944), 966.

of the committee consisted in either expelling undesirable persons from the state or preventing their landing on arrival. One member of the committee described its method thus: "The Committee sent a boat aboard every vessel that came in from Australia to look for convicts. We had a list, which we got from some Englishman here, of all the convict ships that went from England to Australia, alphabetically arranged, extending over several years. We examined all the passengers when the ship came in. They were all placed forward, and called into the Cabin one by one, and questions asked as to what year they arrived in Australia, and by what vessel, and so we identified them, and as fast as they were examined, they were sent aft. Those that were convicts we put into a boat alongside, and sent them ashore to the Committee rooms until there was a vessel going to Australia, when we paid their passage and sent them back."[12]

Another characteristic example of the vigilantes' work is contained in a night watch report by the captain of the guard. "Detailed squads of men in twos and threes to watch various suspicious places some supposed and others known to be cribs for sidney men   reports from these confirm previous suspicions but detected nothing in particular . . . Mrs. Fawcett who lives six or seven doors from Pacific Street says that she knows personally all the Sidney men in town and two vessels are now hourly expected having on board some 500 men who are completely organized in their various branches of crime. That they have been sent for from here and are all picked men. That if they are prevented from landing by the authorities they have made arrangements to 'lay off' near the ship with boats and let the men jump over board and swim until they pick them up. That they have their boats all ready and are in hourly expectation of the arrival of the ship. She also states that they are desperate men thoroughly regardless of human life their own as well as others and have arranged to burn and plunder the town the moment they get ashore and that they have told her that in less than six

12 Williams, *History*, 234.

months they have numbers enough sufficient to take the town and that in that time they will have full possession."[13]

To make its work more successful in such contingencies, the committee resolved to inform all shipmasters that no convicts were to be landed in California, and that all passengers arriving from penal colonies of Great Britain should possess a certificate of character issued by their government or by the American consul in the port of embarkation. The penalty for the violation of these rules was to be a libel against the ship and a fine against the captain. The Sydney consul pointed out that he did not know every colonist and could not comply with such an order. If California wanted to prevent immigration of convicts or ex-convicts, he suggested, it would have to stop all immigration.[14] Eventually the vigilantes broke up the worst gangs by hanging, incarcerating, or expelling their leaders.

The extralegal and somewhat indiscriminate activity of the Committee of Vigilance and the San Francisco population evoked mixed feelings in Australia, especially after an innocent Australian captain was almost lynched by a mob during a San Francisco fire.[15] The case received great publicity in the Californian and Australian press, and became the occasion for acrimonious debate about the merits and demerits of emigrating to California and about the character of Australians. The American consul in Sydney sided wholeheartedly with the Australians, defending them against the Californian indictments and slanders. The total effect of this argument was a temporary deterioration of American relations with the Australian colonies.[16] The existence of a criminal minority among the Australian immigrants—since it was this minority that appeared in newspaper headlines—was responsible for the bad reputation of their countrymen as a group in California; it, together with other foreign groups, also pro-

[13] Williams, *Papers*, 30.

[14] *Ibid.*, 178, 291, 434, 440, 547; Dispatches, Sydney, II, August 8, 1851.

[15] Williams, *History*, 239ff.

[16] *Ibid.*; *San Francisco Herald*, July 1, 1851; *Sydney Morning Herald*, April 25, August 26, September 1, November 8, 1851; *The Empire*, September 2, 1851; Dispatches, Sydney, II, August 8, September 6, 1851.

vided the first impetus to the rise of antiforeign feeling, which
can still be found in California today.

The existence of gold in Australia had been known since
1823 to a few officials and geologists, but the fact was kept
secret. The government was afraid of the effect a gold rush
might have on a convict population of forty-five thousand,
and also feared that gold digging in Australia would put a
premium on crime in England, changing transportation from
a punishment into a blessing.[17] On several occasions, therefore, colonial governors discouraged the investigation or publication of gold finds.[18] Soon, however, the increasing number
of people who found gold made the secret more difficult to
keep. Furthermore, the drain on manpower from the colonies
to California was aggravating the labor shortage, and an
Australian gold rush would stop the exodus.

The London and colonial governments were in the dilemma
of having to choose between a relatively slow but smooth
development of the colonies at the cost of labor difficulties
and the boom development, with all the attending social
disorders, that would follow the disclosure of the presence of
gold.[19] "What are we to expect," wrote the *London Times*,
"in a second California not separated by a vast Pacific Ocean,
but placed by nature in the very centre of those colonies
which we have selected for the haunts of crime?"[20] Statesmen
and publicists deliberated upon the alternatives. Social conditions in Australia were compared with those in California.
It was decided that life was better organized, more orderly,
and more under proper government control in Australia, so
the effects of a gold rush would probably be less extreme
than in California.[21] Consequently, the government publicized
the discoveries and even sponsored geological investigation.

[17] Roger Therry, *Reminiscences of Thirty Years' Residence in New South
Wales and Victoria* (London, 1863), 369.

[18] *Ibid.*, 368; Ernest Scott, *Short History of Australia* (Oxford, 1927), 207.

[19] Hargraves, *Australia*, 120; *Cambridge History of the British Empire*, VII,
pt. I, 243ff.

[20] September 19, 1851.

[21] *Ibid.*; *Sydney Morning Herald*, July 23, 1851; Dispatches, Sydney, II, May
31, 1851.

The result of this government action was, of course, a gold rush to the fields in New South Wales first and then to the richer areas of Victoria. Diggers from the colonies and nearby islands were soon followed by people from all over the world, but always with a vast majority of Englishmen. Australian emigration to California stopped, and a reverse movement began.[22] With the returning Australians went Americans, about nineteen thousand altogether, between 1851 and 1856. Initially they did not have the sympathy of the colonists, as a result of California's treatment of Australian immigrants. Furthermore, American aggression against Cuba and rumors of American aggressive plans against the Sandwich Islands aroused the suspicions of the colonists.[23]

The American immigrants could be classified broadly into two groups: miners, containing a large minority from California, and merchants. Those who had come from California quickly grew tired of the new country; conditions compared unfavorably with those they had left behind. The gold was hard to dig, water with which to wash the sand was scarce, work with convicts was resented, drinking water and food were limited, health conditions were bad, license fees were high, and there was much friction between Americans and the British citizens. Many parties returned to California, appreciating it now more than before.[24] The American merchant community, however, remained until the boom died down in about 1856, and many influential merchants stayed long beyond that period.

While the Americans were in the colonies they made themselves less obnoxious than their whaling and sealing predecessors. The gold-rush wave of American arrivals was of better quality. The unpleasant elements among them were easily outweighed by the beneficial presence of numerous energetic and respectable merchants. Besides, criminals had less chance of success in Australia than in California. The Australian

---

[22] *Journal des Economistes*, xxx:191 (1851); Dispatches, Sydney, I, January 1, 1850; Soulé, *The Annals*, 405.

[23] Dispatches, Sydney, II, January 1, 1852.

[24] Soulé, *The Annals*, 405.

gold rush was well under government control. Although the miners occasionally considered the use of lynch law, there was never any need to resort to it.[25]

The movements of population between the United States and the Australian colonies were accompanied by movements of goods in the same direction. A considerable flow of trade from Australia to the United States, California in particular, began in 1849. At first almost any goods that could be spared in the colonies were sent, but when the trade became more regular, flour and breadstuffs were the main staples of export. Chilean flour was a strong competitor, but Sydney flour soon acquired a good reputation and therewith a good market in California. The business was extremely profitable. One pound of flour sold for from $5 up to $18 in California.[26] Drafts on London to meet the engagements of the Sydney trade were in great demand in San Francisco.[27]

The climax of Australian shipments to the States was reached in 1850, when eighty-six ships carried goods worth about £95,000. The following year this trade was cut down more than half by the Australian gold rush, and it soon petered out almost completely.[28] The years between 1849 and 1851 were the only period in the history of American-Australian relations during which Australia supplied more goods to America than vice versa. The Australian gold rush quickly made trade flow again in the traditional direction.

Australian gold suddenly made the headlines all over the world. People who had hardly heard of the continent now considered going there to try their luck, while economists soberly estimated the influence of the vast quantities of Australian gold upon the economy of the world. The appearance in Melbourne of an American tourist who "did the world," and allotted thirty days of his precious time to see every part of the continent[29] was final proof that Australia

[25] *London Morning Chronicle,* October 26, 1852.
[26] *New York Herald,* May 25, August 19, September 17, 1849.
[27] *London Times,* October 22, 1850.
[28] Churchward, "Australian-American Relations," 16.
[29] Isabel Massary, *Social Life and Manners in Australia* (London, 1861), 139.

was on the map. Many American businessmen established themselves in Melbourne and Sydney, some on their own, others as representatives of well-known American firms. In Melbourne they all congregated in a quarter of the city around the house of the consul. Every Fourth of July they celebrated for three days, much to the displeasure of the government.[30] They gloried in their reputation as enterprising Yankees. "The Americans appear to maintain their go-ahead character in that country," read a report in *Hunt's Merchant Magazine*.[31] And a French observer stated that initiative, competition, and keen enterprise, everything from which others shied away, they made their special task.[32]

American influence in the development of the two cities, especially in communications, was considerable. Samuel McGowan of Boston built the first magnetic telegraph line on the continent from Melbourne to Geelong at $1000 per mile, and Americans managed the line. Several coach lines between the cities and their suburbs were established by Americans with American coaches. Americans also established a post office, an express office, and a fire brigade, and they were active in the chambers of commerce. They built and owned the best hotels in the country.[33] One American, opening the Criterion in Melbourne, fitted several rooms in the most gaudy colors, with gilded furniture and an abundance of mirrors, and rented these "Digger's Nuptial Suites" for £20 a night. He did a tremendous business. The rooms became such a mark of distinction and object of competition among potential brides that they exacted the promise of a few days' tenancy from their future husbands before agreeing to marriage.[34]

Commerce was flourishing, for several reasons. First, of

---

[30] Alfred Jacobs, "Les Européens dans l'Océanie," *Revue des deux Mondes*, XIX:106 (1859); Dispatches, Melbourne, I, March 4, 1856.

[31] XXXI:747 (1854).

[32] Jacobs, "Les Européens dans l'Océanie," 106.

[33] George Francis Train, *An American Merchant in Europe, Asia, and Australia* (New York, 1857), pt. II; *Hunt's Merchant Magazine*, XXXI:747 (1854).

[34] Henry G. Turner, *A History of the Colony of Victoria* (London, 1904), I:374.

course, there was the increase in population and wealth in the colonies. Second, in 1851 the British Navigation Acts were abolished, facilitating foreign trade with the colonies. Third, New South Wales, and a little later Victoria, eliminated preferential duties and other dues in 1851. Fourth, American shippers had acquired the habit of trading in the Pacific. Fifth, in 1852 California was in a depression and eastern shippers welcomed the alternative market in Australia.

Australian economic affairs now received considerable attention in the American press—a reflection of the growing interest. Exchange rates and exchange procedures were explained for the benefit of exporters, and the establishment of manufacturing plants in Australia was advocated, with the certainty "of amassing fortunes in a short time." Australian trade reports in London papers were reprinted in American papers, since "the hints" they contained might "be of service to shippers in the United States who commenced intercourse with that country."[35]

The first big shipments from America, mostly of food, arrived between May and August 1853. They proved a big loss to their owners and eliminated a number of small merchants. Traders in Australia, especially in Melbourne, had anticipated large demands and famine prices, and had stocked up before May. After one hundred vessels had brought in American goods during those four months, many owners were glad to recover the cost of freight from the sales or to reship the goods to England before they spoiled on the wharfs for lack of storage space.[36]

Warnings from American merchants on the spot had arrived too late to prevent these shipments. When the trade developed into healthier and less speculative channels, it became profitable.[37] American provisions, such as ham, bacon,

[35] *Hunt's Merchant Magazine*, xxviii:496 (1853), xxix:509 (1853), xxxi:393 (1854).

[36] *Ibid.*, xxxii:158ff (1855); *Illustrated London News*, xxiii:127, 359, 463 (1853).

[37] *Hunt's Merchant Magazine*, xxxii:158ff (1855); Dispatches, Sydney, ii, May 31, November 20, 1851, August 13, 1852; Melbourne, i, July 1, November 22, 1854.

butter, cheese, beef, and preserves, furniture, wooden houses, carriages, wagons, and boots were introduced and were well liked. Until Australians could turn again to the pursuit of agriculture and forestry, the market for American flour and lumber remained good. American flour was the most popular in the colonies, and in general, American articles competed successfully with goods from the mother country.[38] Much of this trade ceased after 1855 and its character changed. Yet, during this period a foundation was laid for the continued import of a number of American manufactured articles, and the good will created by successful American merchants at this time was helpful to later American exporters.

The new importance of Australia as a goal for immigrants and a market for export goods called for large amounts of shipping space. This was eventually of great benefit to America because clipper ships became the most popular means of transportation between England and Australia and the United States and Australia. Once a clipper had established a record run of sixty-four days outward and seventy-four days homeward between Liverpool and Melbourne, the competing shipping companies were obliged to acquire clippers; they were the only vessels that could achieve such results. Consequently the demand for clipper ships leaped up-

---

[38] *Hunt's Merchant Magazine,* xxxii:158ff (1855); cf. *ibid.,* xxxiv:420 (1856). To indicate the size of the American-Australian trade at this time, the following statistics are given, gathered from various issues of *Hunt's Merchant Magazine* during the years 1853 to 1856:

	Years ending June			
	1852	*1853*	*1854*	*1855*
U.S. exports to Australia				
Domestic merchandise	$196,554	$4,148,828	$2,999,635	$2,703,043
Foreign merchandise	$ 11,713	$ 138,174	$ 149,444	$ 320,506
Australian exports to U.S.	.....	.....	$ 214,202	$ 223,593
Tonnage entering and clearing U.S.				
ports	.....	75,420	52,752	52,030

These figures do not agree entirely with those given by Churchward, "Australian-American Relations," 17, gleaned from Australian sources. However, they tally sufficiently to give a correct impression of the volume of the trade. *Hunt's Merchant Magazine,* xxxii:159 (1855), published a long letter from an American merchant in Melbourne giving import and export figures which he claimed to have from the most reliable government sources and which differ greatly from those given above. Cf. New South Wales, *Statistical Returns, 1841–1850,* 15, 18, 20, 21; *Statistical Returns, 1837–1852,* 21.

ward, and the superior quality of American-built clippers guaranteed that this demand would be satisfied in American shipyards. Sixty-six clipper ships were launched in American yards in 1852, and one hundred and twenty-five in 1853. Many of these were used on runs to Australia.[39]

As steamers replaced sailing vessels, the American consuls urged the need for steamship communication between the colonies and the United States for the improvement of relations between them. New South Wales was even willing to contribute a subsidy of £6000 per year.[40] Finally in 1853 the Australian Steamship Line was established in New York, and the first attempt was made to inaugurate a regular service between the United States and Australia. A circular route was to be followed between the United States, England, and Australia. Only one run was made, however. The British post office refused to pay for the carrying of mails, expenses were too high, and there was insufficient cargo from Australia to the States—a condition from which all shipping lines at that time were suffering. A second American attempt to establish a line with Australian participation was frustrated by the favoritism shown by the British government to British lines, much against the desires of the Australians, who complained about neglect from the mother country and were favorably inclined toward Americans.[41] When the gold boom subsided, interest in shipping lines subsided with it.

The two gold rushes established a sudden and somewhat frantic relationship between the United States and Australia. Not all the contacts created during that period were desirable, and many were undone again. A healthy nucleus remained, however, which was the beginning of mutually beneficial relations that lasted into more quiet days.

[39] Dispatches, Melbourne, I, May 4, 1858; Sydney, IV, October 11, 1858; Arthur H. Clark, *The Clipper Ship Era* (New York, 1910), chaps. XVII, XVIII; Carl C. Cutler, *Greyhounds of the Sea* (New York, 1930), II:251, 280; Eldon Griffin, *Clippers and Consuls* (Ann Arbor, 1938), 18.

[40] Dispatches, Sydney, II, May 31, September 6, 1851; Melbourne, I, July 1, 1854.

[41] Churchward, "Australian-American Relations," 21, 22; *London Times*, April 15, 1856.

CHAPTER V

American Precedents in Australian Politics

THE vanguard of America's penetration into the Pacific was the Far Eastern merchant and fisherman of New England. They appeared in China, Australia, India, the Sandwich Islands, and the Pacific South American states immediately after independence was achieved. But much time passed before Pacific countries felt the full impact of American power. The expansive forces of the industrial age which drove Europeans to look overseas for raw materials, markets, and adventures turned the attention of Americans toward the vast emptiness of their own continent. The mentality of imperialism was present in America as much as it was in Europe; the difference was that in America it could express itself within national borders. Only the groups whose livelihood depended on the oceans sensed the importance of the Pacific. Thanks to their persistence, enterprise, and pressure upon the government, Congress and the Navy began to consider America's position in the Pacific.

An expedition in 1812 was frustrated only by the war with England, and was eventually sent in 1835. American consuls were appointed to nurse growing commerce; in 1822 to Hawaii, in 1834 to Tahiti, in 1845 to Samoa, in addition to those sent to China and Australia. President Tyler in December 1842 and President Taylor in December 1849 referred in general terms to American interests in the Pacific. American missionaries could be found in many Pacific islands, and they tried their best to arouse public interest in their work. But still the little interest the American public saved for external affairs was directed mostly toward the Atlantic and countries beyond. Then the gold rush and the growing population in California turned the attention and imagination of the American people in a different direction. A number of events occurred, in part a consequence of the gold rush, in part simply coincidence, which brought home to Americans the great possibilities of their own West and the Pacific Ocean.

Commodore Perry opened Japan to foreign intercourse. As the "first American imperialist," he suggested somewhat prematurely the acquisition of "a sufficient number of ports of refuge" in the Pacific for the protection of American commerce.[1] The Panama railroad across the isthmus was opened, stimulating commerce to the Pacific. American missionaries appeared in the Pacific islands in increasing numbers, as did merchants. The completion of the transcontinental railroad and the improvement of shipping facilities brought the people of the East Coast closer to the Pacific. The ocean ceased to be a somewhat mysterious body of water, the playground of explorers, adventurous traders, and tough sailors. The first stage in the assertion of American influence in the Pacific was completed: the people knew of the Pacific.

The development of Australian interest in the Pacific was similar, though easier to achieve. The first decades in the life of the original colony were absorbed by the task of making human existence possible. Exploration followed. Both efforts were directed inland. But the need of water communication with the homeland and among the widely separated settlements of the colonies themselves maintained an oceanic outlook in the inhabitants.[2] Interest in conditions of the Pacific could not, for these reasons alone, remain asleep for long. In Australia too the gold rush precipitated an evolution which had roots in an earlier period. Most important in this change was the influx of free immigrants, altering the character of the population. The new arrivals resented the continued use of the colonies as penal establishments and soon succeeded in their agitation against the transportation system. Transportation ceased in 1850 to New South Wales, in 1852 to Tasmania, and in 1868 to Western Australia.

A factor of basic importance for the future of the colonies was the fact that most of the gold-rush immigrants were

[1] W. S. Rossiter, "The First American Imperialist," *North American Review*, CLXXXII: 244 (1906).

[2] *Cambridge History of the British Empire*, VII, pt. I, 342.

British. The census of 1861 showed only 7.6 per cent of the population to be non-British. The ties between the colonists and the mother country remained, therefore, extremely close. "Home News" from England had first place in the colonial press. Notwithstanding a separation of thousands of miles, colonists shared the joys and fears of the British with almost equal intensity,[3] a phenomenon which must be remembered for a satisfactory explanation of Australian attitudes.

Another important factor in the new immigration was the European background of the forties which the new citizens brought with them. The demand for self-government, for decent standards of living, for social legislation, became irresistible with their arrival.[4] A third event of outstanding importance during the gold-rush period was the rapid transformation of gold production from easy digging into an industry. This meant a mutation in the colonial economy with a consequent need for adjustment by a large part of the population; they changed essentially from an independent position to the status of laborers. Also the neglected sheep farming was taken up again and a new interest in agriculture developed, as well as in manufacturing and commerce, including foreign commerce.[5]

The consequence of these major developments in the wake of the gold rush was the formation of a new attitude and perspective of Australians toward themselves, toward their relations to Great Britain, and toward their status as a Pacific people. The outcome was in some cases the result of new conditions, in others merely the logical conclusion of earlier situations. In almost every instance, directly or indirectly, the United States had some influence upon this readjustment, which took place in the fifties and sixties of the nineteenth century.

In the political sphere three major subjects preoccupied the colonists: the relation of the colonies to Great Britain, the

[3] *Ibid.*, 264, 525; "Democratic Government in Victoria," *Westminster Review,* LXXXIX:226 (1868).

[4] *Cambridge History of the British Empire,* VII, pt. I, 270.

[5] *Ibid.*, 262.

internal political organization, and the foreign policy, or more specifically, the defense of the colonies.

The proper relations between the imperial government and the colonies and the amount of freedom to be granted to them had been a vexatious question from the beginning of the settlements. Originally London believed the population needed a rather strong government. This was thoroughly disliked by liberals in Great Britain and the colonies. They began a debate on the whole subject which did not arouse much interest among the early settlers but which led up to the ardent discussions in the middle of the century, when the new-type colonists demanded a more liberal government.

Jeremy Bentham, one of the earliest critics of the colonial government, attacked the autocratic rule of the governor of New South Wales in 1802. He denied the King's power to confer legislative authority upon the governor without a previous sanction of such authority by parliament. Even in America, he pointed out, the Crown had not enjoyed the right to legislate without parliament.[6] A year later, the *Edinburgh Review* carried an article deprecating the whole New South Wales experiment, and pointing out that sooner or later, when the colony grew up, Englishmen would only humble themselves with "a fresh set of Washingtons and Franklins."[7]

Piecemeal criticism of the government continued both in the colony and in England, until in 1819 W. C. Wentworth published a complete treatise on the government of his native colony, New South Wales. In his severe criticism of the tyrannical administration he declared that the settlers would not long tolerate the oppression. Had the British government learned nothing from the "terrible" lesson of the American colonies, now competitors and enemies instead of friends and supporters? The colonists might easily be goaded into open rebellion for independence; they might be driven to approach the United States by a desire to place themselves under "more just and considerate" rulers, or to throw themselves

---

[6] *A Plea for the Constitution* . . . (London, 1803), secs. IV, V.
[7] II:32 (1805).

into the arms of such a powerful protector.[8] This idea was somewhat naive, but it indicated the readiness of the colonists—which had shown itself before and was to show itself more often in the future—to use the United States as a lever to force concessions from the mother country, and it also indicated the close attention the colonists paid to American conditions.

Reference to the possibility of independence after the American precedent continued to be made so often as to permit the conclusion that the thought was ever present in the minds of the colonists. In 1820 the chief justice of New South Wales, Barron Field, warned the royal commissioner Bigge, apropos a petition by the emancipists for an improved legal and economic status, that he could "see the shadow of the spirit of the American revolt at taxation, rising in the shape of a petition for trial by jury; it will next demand a legislative assembly, and end in declaring itself a nation of freebooters and pirates."[9]

The question of independence was brought up as an important argument again when the debate over imperial relations and the colonial government became most acute between 1850 and 1860. To many the political agitation in the colonies appeared to be an exact parallel to American pre-revolution days. Englishmen, anxious to avoid a separation, warned the government that "the mismanagement and overbearing blundering" of the governor were causing discontent and irritation among the colonial population like that prevailing in America just before the revolution.[10] One writer advocated the creation of an hereditary aristocracy in the colony because he felt the existence of such a class, maintaining contact with the Crown and with their equals in England, would have prevented the American revolution.[11]

[8] *Statistical, Historical and Political Description of the Colony of New South Wales* (London, 1819), 164, 243, 244, 245.

[9] Quoted by A. W. Jose, *Builders and Pioneers of Australia* (London, 1928), 46.

[10] Hansard, *Parliamentary Debates*, cviii:567ff (1850); Victoria, *Parliamentary Debates*, ix:2140 (1869); *Illustrated London News*, xvii:470 (1850).

[11] "Political and Social Prospects of the Australian Colonies," *Fraser's Magazine*, lvii:669 (1858).

These thoughts on separation after the American model were not just idle speculations; a number of prominent colonists enthusiastically advocated complete independence. One of the most ardent supporters of separation by peaceful means was the Reverend J. D. Lang. His main arguments were the incompatibility of imperial government with liberty, the danger into which the colony might be plunged by a metropolitan foreign policy upon which the colonists had no influence, and the reduced material benefits for mother country and colony alike if dependence was to continue.[12] Lang's writings and pamphlets as well as those of his disciples drew liberally upon the American experience for telling points and illustrations. His polemics leave little doubt about the influence of Thomas Paine, Patrick Henry, and James Otis upon his thought.[13] Yet though Lang and his friends were men of renown, their ideas did not strike root. Their followers adhered to them personally rather than to their principles.[14] Nevertheless their campaign was important as a contribution to the clarification and elaboration of arguments relating to imperial relations. The separatist propaganda, intellectually much indebted to American revolutionary thought, stimulated thinking and discussion in the colonies, eventually conducing to a development of the imperial connection along more liberal lines.

The second major political problem, government in the colonies, was hardly separable from the question of imperial relations. The gist of this debate was a demand for self-government.[15] Here, too, early agitation by a few colonists had prepared the field for the main battles fought in the fifties and sixties. Under Wentworth's leadership the struggle began early in the century. Step by step the British government made concessions to colonial demands until in the fifties the main aspects of the issue were settled. Responsible govern-

---

[12] Many Englishmen agreed to this last point.

[13] Cf. Henry L. Hall, *Australia and England* (London, 1934), chap. IV.

[14] *Illustrated London News*, XVII:199 (1850).

[15] About the misunderstanding over "self-government" versus "responsible government" see *Cambridge History of the British Empire*, VII, pt. I, chap. X.

ment was introduced in New South Wales, Victoria, and Tasmania in 1855, in South Australia in 1856, and in Queensland in 1859.[16] The main basis of these new governments was an act of parliament in 1850, which through the liberty it granted to the colonies opened an era of great legislative activity. The act itself had drawn a framework for government and had given wide authority for constitutional change. The colonies immediately attacked the difficult task of filling in the details and giving themselves new constitutions to their own taste.[17]

The constitutional debates in all the colonies except Western Australia referred constantly to the United States. Comparisons between the colonies and the United States forced themselves upon many legislators' minds because conditions in the two areas seemed very similar. The settlements were new, the population was sparse and unused to self-government, foreign affairs were entirely secondary, no kings or princes oppressed the freedom of the individual.[18] Wentworth, for instance, frequently turned for authority and precedent to "those States the name of which was in every man's mouth in reference to the constitution fitted for this colony: I mean the United States of America."[19] In the Queensland Legislative Council one official almost complained about the frequent quoting of the American constitution in their debates.[20] Other legislators found American precedents entirely inapplicable to their colonies. The character of the soil, the economy, the composition and background of the population differed in the two countries; so these legislators refused to follow the American model, using it only to demonstrate its

[16] *Official Year Book of the Commonwealth of Australia*, XI:p. xxxiv (1918).
[17] For details see *Cambridge History of the British Empire*, VII, pt. I, chap. X; A. C. V. Melbourne, *Early Constitutional Development in Australia* (London, 1934), pt. V.
[18] Hansard, *Parliamentary Debates*, CIX:1314ff (1850); *London Times*, February 13, 1850.
[19] New South Wales, Parliament, Legislative Council, *The Speeches in the Legislative Council of New South Wales on the Second Reading of the Bill for Framing a New Constitution for the Colony* (Sydney, 1853), 26.
[20] Queensland, *Parliamentary Debates*, XI:167f (1870).

inapplicability to their own circumstances. But even they used it, though negatively.[21]

There was hardly any issue in connection with which the American example was not cited. American experience was scrutinized with regard to such important questions as constitutional amendment clauses, decentralization of government, creation of administrative areas, and composition of an upper house—and also to such secondary questions as free railroad travel for new immigrants.[22]

In spite of such close observation of the American political system, and although there was hardly a legislative meeting without some mention of American institutions, the colonists prided themselves on their close adherence to traditional British concepts. They devoted themselves with great passion and fervor to the English connection, and were quite sensitive to any reproach of deviation therefrom. The charge of "Americanization" was "the most telling sarcasm" that could be used against the colonists.[23] And there is no conclusive proof that the American example was merely imitated in the framing of any colonial constitution. Nevertheless, from the careful attention which colonial statesmen, legislatures, and newspapers paid to American political conditions in the fifties and sixties, considerable American influence upon Australian political organization can easily be recognized. Whether the American model was used as an example to be emulated or to be discarded, it helped in the shaping of the Australian polity.

In the third major political problem of this period, foreign policy and especially defense, the United States also appeared much in the discussions of the colonists. The interest of the colonists in their foreign relations was, however, as yet very limited. Their few contacts with foreign nations could easily

[21] E.g., "Political and Social Prospects of the Australian Colonies," 665; Victoria, *Parliamentary Debates*, i:181f, 330 (1866); ix:2140, 2143 (1869); Queensland, *Parliamentary Debates*, xi:167f (1870); *London Times*, February 19, 1850.

[22] Queensland, *Parliamentary Debates*, i:121 (1864); ix:121 (1869); xi:167f (1870); New South Wales, Parliament, *The Speeches in the Legislative Council*, 26, 30, 38, 56ff.

[23] "Democratic Government in Victoria," 226.

be taken care of by the mother country. The great colonial debates around 1870 over the status of the colonies when the mother country should be at war showed clearly that the colonists were content to let London handle their foreign relations. Somewhat illogically, they restricted their concern to the military security of the colonies. Sensitivity, stemming from the lonely and exposed position of the colonies, and born almost simultaneously with the settlements, continued to dominate colonial thinking in the second half of the nineteenth century. But now, with nationalism growing and foreign contacts increasing, this fear of aggression found more than sporadic expression.

Newly established relations between the colonies and neighboring islands in the Pacific added a material basis to the earlier political claim of the colonies to hold sway over the territories in their region. Australian missionaries covered a wide area around the continent, and colonists had settled in many nearby islands. Australian merchants had established a fairly regular and profitable trade with Pacific islands and China. Sydney shippers provided the carrying facilities. As is well known, the commercial representatives of the colonies behaved very badly toward the natives in the western Pacific. Not only was their trade conducted in a most cruel manner, but they also dealt in natives for ship crews and carried on what amounted to a slave trade for the sugar cane fields of Queensland. This trade in men and goods was reckless and lawless because most of the islands were outside the jurisdiction of any colonial power.[24]

The colonists had thus reasons of security, of trade, and of humanitarianism for preventing the islands from falling into the hands of a foreign power. As a result, mutually antagonistic groups favored and agitated for the annexation of many of the Pacific islands by Great Britain. Missionaries, driven by humanitarian motives, and almost at war with the un-

[24] John G. Paton, *An Autobiography* (New York, 1889), I: 183ff; John E. Erskine, *Journal of a Cruise among the Islanders of the Western Pacific* (London, 1853), 13, 15, 18f, 486ff; Ramsay Muir, *A Short History of the British Commonwealth* (New York, 1924), 11, 539; *London Times*, November 2, 1870.

scrupulous merchants of colonial and other origin, demanded the establishment of British jurisdiction over the islands for the sake of law and order. They either appealed directly to the government, or caused their native converts to appeal to the "Great Chief of Sydney" for protection.[25]

The more materialistically minded shippers and traders of Sydney and Melbourne made similar appeals for different reasons. They feared that other nations might anticipate British annexation and thus destroy their trade. Their anxiety was particularly great with regard to the Fiji Islands following the American Civil War. Cotton was short in the United States and was grown at the time in the Fijis by Australian and American immigrants. The United States might want to annex the islands.[26] Besides, the colonists feared the United States might want these islands and some others for "the convenience of having a good footing in the Pacific" for strategic purposes.[27]

The Reverend Lang promptly introduced a formal petition in the New South Wales legislature calling for the colony's dominion over the Fijis. He pressed for action because the North German Federation and the United States were already reported "to have been nibbling."[28] An intercolonial conference at Melbourne in 1870 repeated the demand, but neither Lang nor the conference could induce the British government to act. The following year the New South Wales government again requested annexation of the Fijis, and received the disappointing answer that England was interested in these islands only to the degree that the Australian colonies were interested, and if New South Wales desired to annex the islands the British government would not object.

[25] Paton, *Autobiography*, I: 367.

[26] *Melbourne Age*, November 5, 1870. Some American settlers presented a petition demanding a protectorate by the United States to their vice-consul, who received it enthusiastically. The American government stated officially, however, that it had no intention of declaring a protectorate over the Fijis. Guy H. Scholefield, *The Pacific, Its Past and Future* (London, 1919), 85; Dispatches, Sydney, VI, May 30, 1868, November 5, 1869; Melbourne, III, February 18, 1868; *Melbourne Argus*, February 7, 1868; *Sydney Morning Herald*, June 23, 1868.

[27] *London Times*, December 27, 1870.

[28] *Ibid.*

However, the appalling conditions in the islands and the constant pressure from the colonies finally impelled Great Britain to annex the Fijis in 1874.[29]

Annexation of the Pacific islands for security reasons found the widest popular support in the colonies. There was almost unanimous agreement that peace could not be assured until the islands in the Australian Pacific region were under British control. Yet, in the fifties and sixties colonial feeling on this point had not yet reached its apex, although the extreme reluctance of the British government toward annexations was already causing much ill feeling in the colonies.[30]

The most likely explanation for the extraordinary nervousness of the Australian colonies about their security lies in their close sentimental ties with England. Every time Great Britain was threatened with war or was actually at war, the colonies were deeply involved mentally, and also physically through the precautionary measures they took to guard against attacks.[31] With some envy Australians looked to the United States, which seemed so secure behind its water barriers—barriers that to them seemed to offer no protection.[32] With such a psychological attitude, it is not surprising that even in peacetime Australians were perennially concerned with their defense and looking for the potential aggressor—at this time usually France and the United States, but later Germany and Japan—against whom protection was needed. Repeatedly in this period American military attacks were at least hypothetically envisaged, while growing American

[29] *Ibid.*, September 5, 19, 1870; December 2, 1871; *Cambridge History of the British Empire*, VII, pt. I, 352.

[30] This was especially true when France annexed New Caledonia in 1853; see Walter Murdoch, *Alfred Deakin* (London, 1923), 112ff; Muir, *Short History*, 539, 633f; Henri Merens, *Etude sur les colonies Anglaises autonomes de l'Australie et du Canada* (Toulouse, 1907), 63ff.

[31] Hansard, *Parliamentary Debates*, CC:1824 (1870); cf., for the situation during the Crimean War, *Illustrated London News*, XXIV:501, XXV:59 (1854); during Anglo-French tension in 1859, *Cambridge History of the British Empire*, VII, pt. I, 344; during the American Civil War, Hall, *Australia and England*, 106ff; during the Franco-German war, Victoria, *Parliamentary Debates*, X:686, XI:732, 754 (1870); *London Times*, November 2, 1870; *et al.*

[32] Hall, *Australia and England*, 105; Dispatches, Melbourne, IV, March 28, 1871.

influence in the Pacific began to disturb Australian minds much more concretely.

The danger of England's involvement in the American Civil War again stirred up considerable anxiety in the Australian colonies. The privateers from the War of 1812 were not forgotten. Sir Charles Gavan Duffy in the Victorian legislature remarked that it would be impossible for Victoria to provide for its own defense against such an aggressor as the United States, for instance, which was powerful enough to do great injury to the colony.[33] And during another scare in 1870 Duffy referred to the great contest of the powers for control of the seas. He minimized Britain's predominance in the face of the American and French challenge and questioned whether the British fleet could protect Australian ports against fleets stationed in New Caledonia or San Francisco.[34]

Fortunately the question was never put to a practical test. The basic trust of the colonists in the overwhelming power of the British Navy remained unshaken, and friendly relations with America continued. In most cases the ideas about potential American aggression were theoretical and were used for ulterior purposes such as to create sympathy in Australia for neutrality or defense expenditures. Few people in the colonies really believed in a war between Great Britain and the United States at that time. Certainly the readiness of Australians to make contacts with the United States and their admiration for American institutions was proof of their friendly disposition.

If further proof was needed, it was provided with the arrival of the Confederate cruiser *Shenandoah* in Melbourne in 1865. Diplomatically the presence of the steamer in Australian waters created some complications concerning British neutrality and even led to friction between Victoria and the mother country.[35] The population of the colony, however,

[33] Victoria, *Parliamentary Debates*, IX:2165 (1869).

[34] *Ibid.*, X:686 (1870); cf. Hansard, *Parliamentary Debates*, CC:1823 (1870).

[35] United States Navy Department, *Official Records of the Union and Confederate Navies in the War of the Rebellion* (Washington, 1896), ser. 1, III: 759ff; Victoria, *Parliamentary Debates*, XV:2309 (1872); Dispatches, Melbourne, III, February 23, 1865.

was unhampered by the political or legal aspects of the visit and used it for a demonstration of friendliness which one of the cruiser's officers described as baffling all description.[36] The crew became the "little lions" of Melbourne. Their stay was one continuous festival, and the officers confessed that the Melbourne ladies gave them the best time they had ever had in their lives. The only dark spot was an occasional argument or fist fight with some Yankees, who were even suspected of attempting to sabotage the vessel.[37]

The colonists' speculations on security and defense were not new in principle. Fear of aggression in the early days of the New South Wales settlement and the statement of policy in the *Sydney Gazette* of 1827 were based on like considerations. In the same vein Wentworth's last words when he left Australia in 1854 were that he would pray for the happiness of his people and for its rapid expansion into a nation which should rule supreme in the southern world.[38] This was Australia's "manifest destiny." It had been announced before, and was to be much more actively pursued in the future. In this period, though, the penetration of western powers increasingly deeper into what Australians considered their particular sphere of interest and influence gave to the colonies' military and strategic problems more reality and urgency. To Australians the danger from imperialist ambitions of other nations seemed to change from a potential threat into an actual peril. The United States as one of these nations thus became instrumental in the crystallization of an Australian policy designed to counteract foreign activity and to assert Australia's leading status in the western Pacific. The first success of this Australian policy was Great Britain's deference to colonial wishes in the Fiji affair. This event was an early indication that, small as the influence of the Australian colonies might be, Australian opinion could not be ignored by those with interests in the Pacific.

[36] Cornelius E. Hunt, *The Shenandoah* (New York, 1867), 95, 101, 106, 110.

[37] *Ibid.;* see also the contemporary *London Times* and *New York Times*. Visits of American Navy ships to Australian ports were quite frequent. Dispatches, Sydney, i, January 1, 1840; Melbourne, x, October 16, 1885.

[38] *Sydney Morning Herald*, March 21, 1854.

In the economic sphere also American influence continued
to make itself felt in the fifth and sixth decades of the nineteenth century, both as an example for economic legislation
and in commercial relations. American influence upon economic legislation was not pronounced, however, because of
the great disparity in economic conditions. Australia was
mainly in the pastoral stage, whereas the United States had
developed agriculture and manufacturing. Where an American pioneer could support himself with a small farm, the
Australian must own large areas of grazing land to make
sheep farming successful. Australians maintained in the
middle of the century that their land was strictly limited,
whereas it was abundant in the United States. The basis for
effective land legislation, of eminent importance in the colonies, was therefore considered entirely different, and American precedents were of no value to the Australian colonists,
at least according to the prevailing opinion in the colonial
legislatures.[39] In the debates about free trade the situation
in the two countries was acknowledged to be more similar.
However, both the proponents and the enemies of free trade
seemed to find arguments from American precedents, so that
the American experience did not offer any convincing evidence for a desirable choice to the colonists.[40]

In a more concrete and successful way American-Australian
economic relations were maintained by the American merchants and entrepreneurs who survived the gold-rush boom.
They maintained a thin but steady flow of various American
goods into Australia. Especially after the opening of the
transcontinental railroad Americans looked for an increase
in trade to Australia,[41] but their hopes were never quite

[39] Victoria, *Parliamentary Debates*, IX:2152 (1869); "Political and Social
Prospects of the Australian Colonies," 665; "Democratic Government in Victoria," 239.

[40] E.g., Victoria, *Parliamentary Debates*, I:181f (1866). Australians envied
the support which the federal government gave to the states for the maintenance
of agricultural colleges. In this period, also, the United States exchanged seeds
with the Melbourne Botanical Gardens. Cf. Brian Fitzpatrick, *The British Empire
in Australia* (Melbourne, 1941), 213.

[41] *London Times*, December 2, 1871; Dispatches, Sydney, VI, August 31, 1867,
December 4, 1868.

fulfilled because Australia lacked export articles of interest to the States. The only item of importance was coal, which was sent in large quantities to the West Coast. While it may be interesting to note that Australia sent some pig iron to the United States, and shipped agricultural machines there before the more normal reverse trend was established, economically these shipments were of little significance.[42] The Australian staple, wool, never found a large market in America in spite of the fact that American buyers made a strong bid to divert some of the Australian wool trade from London to San Francisco.[43] The few shipments which went to America were a result of extraordinary circumstances following the Civil War. A senator dashed the hope of Californians by calling the idea that the United States might go to Australia for wool an absurdity.

Americans had a not inconsiderable share in the internal economic development of the colonies. Especially during the Civil War, when American imports into Australia ceased, American capitalists, experts, and workers participated in the production of some goods formerly imported from the United States. Their advice and help were especially welcome in the growing of cotton and tobacco.[44] Americans also assisted as advisers and suppliers of machinery in the establishment of mining and iron industries.[45] Above all, they continued to pioneer in the development of communications, both overseas and inland. The firm of Cobb and Company was particularly outstanding in this activity. The buggy and the bush-coach, two "instruments of torture," were introduced and eventually fabricated locally by this firm as vehicles well adapted to a territory without roads. Cobb combined the

[42] Fitzpatrick, *The British Empire,* 214; Shann, *An Economic History,* 418; Dispatches, Sydney, IV, October 12, 1858; v, July 2, 1860, April 19, 1862.

[43] *London Times,* December 2, 1871; Victoria, *Parliamentary Debates,* XIII: 1567, XIV:957 (1871). The American tariff against Australian wool was regretted by many Australians and Americans interested in trade between the two areas. Dispatches, Melbourne, I, July 1, 1854; Sydney, I, January 1, 1841.

[44] *Hunt's Merchant Magazine,* XLVII:362 (1862); Queensland, *Parliamentary Debates,* I:219 (1864).

[45] Shann, *An Economic History,* 418, 422. Some of these industries failed.

import and manufacturing business with the transportation business, and soon rose to be the most important transport company on the continent. Its thousands of vehicles on regular routes blazed the trail for the Australian railroads and motor highways, and buggies were used for transportation until as recently as 1924.[46] Other American firms were equally active, though with less success, in running shipping lines between the West Coast and Australia. Their numerous projects usually failed, though, because of lack of cargo and the competition of government-subsidized British shipping lines.[47]

[46] *Ibid.*, 285ff.
[47] *London Times,* October 31, December 2, 1871; *New York Daily Tribune,* January 31, 1871; Dispatches, Sydney, vi, December 4, 1868.

CHAPTER VI

Imperialism in the Southern and Western Pacific

THE last three decades of the nineteenth century brought important changes in the Pacific deeply involving America and Australia. The period was characterized by the spirit of imperialism.[1] Especially the Pacific—the last region in which "backward" areas were available for the insatiable appetite of the western powers—was carefully scanned by European nations for the acquisition of new territory. A brief chronology of the scramble for islands—disregarding those of minor significance—will show how radically political conditions in the Pacific changed between 1870 and 1900.

Great Britain annexed the Fiji Islands in 1874. In 1875 Spain claimed sovereignty over the Caroline Islands. Germany obtained some exclusive rights in Tonga in 1876. In 1878 the United States received the right to establish a naval station in Pago Pago and agreed to mediate between Samoa and a foreign power in case of conflict. The next year Germany and Great Britain also obtained special rights by treaty with Samoa. In 1880 France annexed Tahiti. In 1881 Great Britain annexed Rotumah Island. In 1883 France and Great Britain renewed an understanding about the New Hebrides. In 1884 Great Britain declared a protectorate over a part of New Guinea, and Germany annexed another part in addition to the Bismarck Archipelago. In the same year Great Britain annexed the Louisiade, Woodlark, Long, and Rook islands. In 1885 Germany took possession of the Marshall Islands and hoisted the flag over Yap. In 1886 France established a military post on the New Hebrides, Great Britain annexed Santa Cruz and the Kermadec Islands, and the United States obtained by treaty a port of call on Tonga Island.

[1] See Brookes, *International Rivalry*, passim.

Disposing of such piecemeal acquisitions, Germany and Great Britain signed an agreement in 1886 dividing the western Pacific into two halves, each giving the other partner a free hand in his particular sphere. In 1887 France occupied Wallis Island. In 1888 Great Britain annexed the Christmas Islands against American protests and also the Fanning, Penrhyn, Suwarow, and Cook islands. In 1892 the Gilbert and Ellice islands became a British protectorate, and in 1893 the Solomon Islands were annexed by Great Britain. In 1897 the United States annexed Hawaii. In 1898 Spain ceded the Philippine Islands and Guam to the United States, and in 1899 it sold the Caroline, Pelew, and Mariana islands to Germany. During the same year the United States occupied Wake Island, and Great Britain withdrew from Samoa, leaving the United States and Germany alone there. In 1900 Great Britain established a protectorate over Tonga and annexed Niue.

This invasion of hitherto free areas in the Pacific proved most disturbing to the Australian colonies and, as America's interest in the Pacific grew, to that nation as well. By 1870 gaining exclusive control over the islands in the southern and western Pacific had become a traditional Australian policy. Statements such as "Australia should be the supreme Power in the Southern Pacific" or "The islands of Australasia ought to belong to the people of Australasia" were accepted as a matter of fact.[2] The arrival of western powers, turning the Pacific into "another Europe," was resented by Australians as an intrusion and a threat to their vital interests.[3]

To Americans this region of the Pacific had been of only sporadic interest until about 1870. Since Hawaii had been the western limit of the area in which American policy asserted itself, the Pacific "spheres" of Australia and those of the United States did not overlap. "The early American policy in Asia, meaning merely the policy of early Americans

[2] Hall, *Australia and England*, 231; Victoria, *Parliamentary Debates*, XLIII:137 (1883).

[3] *Ibid.; Annexation, Federation, and Foreign Convicts* (Government Printer, Melbourne, 1884).

for there was no other policy, was purely negative in its origins. It appeared only when there was opposition or obstruction to the trade. Where trade was free there was no policy."[4] With the growth of imperialism everywhere and the penetration of western interests into the Pacific, the American attitude toward that ocean changed. The United States began to insist upon what Secretary of State Blaine called the "Just and necessary influence of the United States in the waters of the Pacific."[5] The exact implications of such an idea were not yet clear in 1870, or even by 1880, but it was obvious that America had begun to implement commercial enterprise by individuals with a political policy in the whole Pacific.

Discounting adventures of individual Americans in some Pacific islands beyond Hawaii, which had romantic rather than political or economic significance,[6] the first substantial interest in responsible government circles appeared about 1868. The acquisition of Alaska, the entrance of European powers into the Pacific, the promising growth of the Pacific states, all had the cumulative effect of awakening official America to the importance of the Pacific Ocean. The Navy, as usual anxious for expansion, urged the development of the Midway Islands; the importance of this step, it said, could not be "over-estimated."[7] The Senate naval committee favored the idea and added to the Navy's reasons—strategy and commerce—the argument that if a European power should appropriate the islands, they might be turned into another Nassau, shielding "Alabamas" and "Floridas" under a neutral flag to destroy American commerce. The islands were ideally situated just where the development of national interests and commerce indicated the greatest need.[8] Congress

[4] Tyler Dennett, *Americans in Eastern Asia* (New York, 1941), 69.

[5] *Congressional Record*, xx, pt. 2:1334 (1889).

[6] For details see James Morton Callahan, *American Relations in the Pacific and the Far East, 1784–1900* (Baltimore, 1901), chap. vi.

[7] *Report of the Secretary of the Navy*, 40th Cong., 3rd Sess., p. xxii (December 7, 1868).

[8] *Report of the Senate Committee on Naval Affairs*, no. 194, 40th Cong., 3rd Sess. (January 28, 1869).

followed the committee's advice, and appropriated $50,000 for harbor improvements. This sum proved entirely insufficient and the project was abandoned, although the United States continued to hold the islands.

The debates and reports referring to the Midway Islands indicated clearly that American statesmen were preoccupied with the north Pacific. Consideration was given only to communications with China and Japan. Official concern obviously followed trade. This remained true a few years later, in the early seventies, when American traders in the south Pacific became vocal. Then the American government began to develop a policy for that region also. The initiative came from William H. Webb, the shipowner and shipbuilder from New York. Webb had done some trading in the Pacific during the Civil War and was struck by the commercial possibilities in the southern and western Pacific. He decided to establish a shipping line connecting the United States with the South Sea Islands and Australasia, and applied for a subsidy to Congress in 1870.[9]

Some officials in the government supported this scheme. The American minister resident in Hawaii, Mr. Peirce, had observed the English shipping line between Hawaii and Australasia and was impressed by its success. He recommended to the secretary of state that Webb be granted a subsidy, so the State Department was sympathetic to the project.[10] The Committee on Post Offices and Post Roads also favored it, and the chairman, Senator Ramsey from Minnesota, sup-

[9] Report of the Postmaster General, *House Exec. Doc. No. 1*, pt. 4, 42nd Cong., 2nd Sess., p. xiv (November 18, 1871); *House Exec. Doc. No. 161*, 44th Cong., 1st Sess.:2 (May 1, 1876); *Congressional Record*, xx, pt. 2:1326 (1889). Simultaneously with Webb the American consul in Sydney, Hall, planned a steamship line between Australia and the United States. The competition between the two, combined with intercolonial jealousies, led to a complicated situation which was straightened out after a few years by Hall's obtaining a contract from the New South Wales government. See Dispatches, Sydney, vii, January 28, July 18, December 31, 1870; January 20, May 4, July 1, August 31, December 21, 1871; February 16, March 16, May 23, June 5, September 27, October 24, 1872; February 3, May 16, 1873.

[10] George H. Ryden, *The Foreign Policy of the United States in Relation to Samoa* (New Haven, 1933), 46.

ported a bill granting a subsidy to Webb's steamship line. However, Congress failed to act on the bill before adjournment.[11] When, toward the end of 1871, Congress reconvened, the postmaster general recommended the subsidy, saying the commercial importance of a shipping line between the United States and Australia was beyond question, and traffic would be heavy and beneficial.[12] The following year the President himself recommended the subsidy.[13] Clearly, Webb must have used some convincing arguments to gain sympathy in such high places. However, he failed to win over Congress, for the subsidy was not granted.

The exact reason for this failure cannot be stated with certainty. There was no popular support for the project, and in Congress there still prevailed a reluctance to embark upon any policy leading to expansion beyond national frontiers.[14] But in this case there were also specific reasons. Mr. Webb's application for a subsidy was not the only one; many shipowners and shipbuilders were asking for subsidies for a great number of schemes. Washington was flooded with lobbyists. On the other hand, some shipping interests were opposed to subsidies for reasons of their own. The press was equally divided, partly on principle and partly because the success of the shipping lines was controversial. There was no sense, one expert wrote, in creating with the help of money from the Treasury "a parcel of puffy, bloated enterprises composed of steamboats running hither and thither, for the sole benefit of those who own and run them." The great number of demands for subsidies, their size, and their doubtful merit were responsible for the refusal of Congress to grant them.[15]

[11] *Congressional Globe*, 1871, January 12, p. 452, 19, p. 595, 27, p. 774.

[12] Report of the Postmaster General, *House Exec. Doc. No. 1*, pt. 4, 42nd Cong., 2nd Sess., p. xiv (November 18, 1871).

[13] *House Exec. Doc. No. 1*, pt. 1, 42nd Cong., 3rd Sess., p. xvii (December 2, 1872).

[14] Ryden, *The Foreign Policy*, 47. This attitude did not prevent the granting of a subsidy for a shipping line to the Mediterranean, and the Senate committee was reported to be not unfriendly to subsidies in general. *Senate Report No. 316*, 41st Cong., 3rd Sess. (January 26, 1871).

[15] *New York Daily Tribune*, January 27, 28, February 4, 1871.

The important result of the episode was that Webb had succeeded in directing the attention of the State Department, the Post Office, and important Senate committees to the hitherto neglected areas of the Pacific, at the same time that the Navy had become interested in them. This achievement was only a beginning, though, and could lead to tangible results only after Congress was won over. To this task Webb and his friends devoted themselves, in the meantime not neglecting their steamship project.

Webb had another financial resource in reserve: the New Zealand government had offered him a small subsidy. Webb had refused to accept it pending the outcome of his application to the American government. When he failed in America he accepted the New Zealand money, and in 1871 his line was established, running one steamer monthly from San Francisco via Hawaii to New Zealand and Australia.[16] The new line of communication made the New Zealanders very happy. They had always wanted a line to England via America because this route shortened the trip by about two weeks compared to the usual route via Suez or the Cape of Good Hope.[17] But the subsidy proved to be a heavy burden for the small colony, and the government turned to the Australian colonies with a request for support. Heated discussions in all the colonial parliaments followed this request. Overseas communications were vital to the colonies, and debates over them had gone on with more or less vehemence almost from the establishment of the first colony.

Since the gold rush a number of irregular steamship lines had connected the United States and Australia, but these had disappeared with the boom. During an intercolonial conference in 1867 Queensland and Victoria expressed their desire for a reliable, regular line via the United States.[18] The new request by New Zealand became the subject of another intercolonial conference which carefully scrutinized the three

[16] Report of the Postmaster General, *House Exec. Doc. No. 1*, pt. 4, 42nd Cong., 2nd Sess., p. xiv (November 18, 1871).

[17] *Ibid.*; Victoria, *Parliamentary Debates*, xiii:1563 (1871).

[18] *Ibid.*, 1560.

possible routes between Australia and England: via Suez, the Cape of Good Hope, and the United States. Agreement was reached on a recommendation to subsidize the routes via Suez and the United States.[19]

The strongest support for a United States route came from Victoria because, so the argument ran, the colony's social and economic ties with the United States fully justified the expense. The Victorian government in 1871 decided to become a partner in the agreement with Webb, following the conference recommendation.[20] However, a new government in 1872 took the opposite view and refused to ratify the agreement. This led to an excited debate in the Victorian parliament, dividing the house into two camps.

The government and its supporters maintained that a subsidy should not be granted because (1) the line was of little use as a mail route; (2) there was little traffic to the United States; (3) the required subsidy of £32,500 was too high— the most optimistic figure on mail receipts was only £2500, and the total subsidy for the Suez route, providing communication all the way to Europe, was only £22,000; (4) the subsidy would bring a competitor into the Pacific island trade; (5) for strategic reasons British ships and sailors should be supported because Great Britain and the United States might one day be at war. The other camp favored a subsidy because the line (1) would stimulate trade with America; (2) would open a new market in the Pacific islands for the growing colonial manufacturing; (3) would stimulate immigration into Australia; (4) would provide a safe route when England was at war with a European power. To these arguments Webb added his own in the form of his glamorous steamer *Nebraska*, which he showed off in Australian ports.[21]

Thus both groups appealed to considerations of economy, public interest, security, and patriotism for their opposing views. Eventually the motion against the subsidy was carried.[22] Similar debates took place in some of the other col-

---

[19] *Ibid.*, 1555.   [20] *Ibid.*, 1557; xiv:742 (1872).
[21] *London Times*, December 2, 1871.
[22] Victoria, *Parliamentary Debates*, xiv:938ff (1872); xv:1942ff (1872).

onies, but were considerably less intense. Outside Victoria interest in a route via America was smaller because close ties with the United States were lacking, and because steamers would call at other ports only after they had called at Melbourne—an important point in the intercolonial jealousies.[23]

The unfavorable decisions by Congress and the Australian parliaments failed to stop the steamers of Webb's United States, New Zealand, and Australia Mail Steamship Company from plying between America, New Zealand, and Australia. Webb actively engaged in expanding his business and improving his line, encouraged no doubt by the funds of the New Zealand government and the potentialities of a sympathetic attitude in high places of the American government. During the summer of 1871 he sent Captain E. Wakeman as an agent to Samoa to investigate the possibilities of establishing a coaling station and incidentally to investigate trade opportunities.[24]

Wakeman's report to his principal was enthusiastic on all counts: harbor facilities, commercial opportunities, and a naval station for the United States.[25] His mission turned out to be one of the main stimuli to the expansion of American political interests from the north into the south Pacific. Another indication of increasing American concern over conditions in the southern Pacific was an official reaction to rumors about German plans in Samoa.[26] Finally, the presence of three Navy vessels in the south Pacific in 1870 and 1871 for the purpose of examining and protecting American commerce and interests showed that this area had not been ignored by the government.[27]

Among the Navy ships was the cruiser *Narragansett* under Commander Meade. Following orders from his flagship under Admiral Winslow and provided with a letter by Mr. Peirce in Hawaii, telling him among other things that "in

[23] *Ibid.*, XIII:1560 (1871); Queensland, *Parliamentary Debates*, XI:235 (1870).
[24] *House Exec. Doc. No. 161*, 44th Cong., 1st Sess., 7 (May 1, 1876).
[25] *Ibid.*
[26] Ryden, *The Foreign Policy*, 52ff.   [27] *Ibid.*, 55ff.

view of the future domination of the U. States in the N. & S. Pacific Oceans; it is very important that the Navigator islands should be under American control," Meade sailed for the Samoa Islands, and in 1872 signed a treaty with the chief of Pago Pago, giving the United States considerable influence over these islands.[28]

From the facts of the enterprise it is clear that the plan originated in Honolulu, and was the work of minister-resident Peirce, Admiral Winslow, Webb, and his agent Wakeman. But their action was quite compatible with the attitude prevailing among members of the Administration in Washington. Indeed, the State and Navy departments liked Meade's treaty, and President Grant sent it to the Senate with a recommendation for ratification. The State Department, in a letter to Webb, confirmed its interest in any measure stimulating commerce in the Pacific, either with the Far East or with the newer and growing colonies of Australia and New Zealand, and assured him of a sympathetic consideration of his shipping line and the harbor of Pago Pago.[29]

The Senate never ratified Meade's treaty. The Administration's views on America's status in the southern and western Pacific were ahead of Congress and public opinion. Perhaps Mr. Webb and his friends had a somewhat one-sided influence upon the government, which overlooked the fact that the total commercial interest of Americans in that region of the Pacific was very limited, and that strategic considerations seemed too farfetched as yet to influence the American people in favor of expansion. Nevertheless, the Meade treaty and its reception at the White House were a beginning, a further step toward a positive American policy in the southern Pacific—directly into the region over which the Australasian colonies claimed predominance.

Webb did not relax. The commercial possibilities and the official support of his projects were too valuable to abandon. He succeeded in having Colonel Steinberger, a mutual friend

[28] *Ibid.*   [29] *Ibid.*, 73.

of his and President Grant's, sent to Samoa as a quasi-personal representative of the President for the investigation of conditions. Steinberger returned from the trip in 1873. His long report was acknowledged by the State Department in a very noncommittal way and no official action followed.

A year later Steinberger returned to Samoa. His position this time was ambiguous—probably purposely so, since the Administration favored a more aggressive policy in Samoa but at the same time realized the absence of congressional support.[30] The State Department seemed not averse to a stronger American influence in Samoa, but wanted to leave the door open for retreat in case the attitude of Congress should make this necessary. The instructions Steinberger received from the State Department were very definite regarding his nonofficial status, but between the lines one can read the department's regret at being unable to be more encouraging. The importance of the Samoa Islands was fully recognized, the department stated, but it was doubtful that such considerations would satisfy the American people that the annexation of the islands was essential for the safety or the prosperity of the United States. So far there had been no indication of any popular feeling that would warrant measures leading toward annexation—an action which would be a reversal of the traditional American policy.[31]

The activities of Steinberger and the American Navy and a demand by Samoans for an American protectorate (probably engineered by some Americans), combined with the aggressive action of Germany in Samoa, aroused the fears of Australasians, especially New Zealanders, who, for geographic reasons, were especially interested in Samoa's fate. Between 1870 and 1875 there was strong colonial agitation for the annexation of Samoa, or at the least for a protectorate, by Great Britain. A petition to this effect was sent to the Queen, and the New Zealand prime minister, fearing a future clash in the southern Pacific between Great Britain

[30] *Ibid.*, chap. IV.
[31] *House Exec. Doc. No. 161*, 44th Cong., 1st Sess., 76 (May 1, 1876).

and either Germany, France, or the United States, also advocated the annexation of Samoa.[32]

The Australian colonies were not so much concerned about Samoa, but agreed in principle with New Zealand and shared that colony's anxieties. The worst premonitions of the Australasian colonies were coming true: The great imperialistic powers were showing unmistakable signs of an intention to penetrate into the southern and western Pacific. The violent reaction in the colonies finally forced the mother country into the annexation of the Fiji Islands, but otherwise little was done to protect the colonies from what they felt was an encirclement by foreign powers.[33] The colonies were even reminded by London that other great powers had good claims to some of the islands, especially Samoa, and that the British authorities would have nothing to do with an Australian Monroe Doctrine.[34]

The apprehensions of the colonies, especially New Zealand's, were somewhat relieved when, between 1877 and 1879, Germany, Great Britain, and the United States made agreements with the Samoans and among themselves tending to put the three powers on an equal footing, thus at least preventing exclusive control by any one of them. The United States was less suspect in the colonies than any other foreign power, and with good reason. Even the most eager American advocates of expansion did not dare to hope that the United States would annex Samoa or any other islands in the southern Pacific. "In my judgment, the U.S. Government is not prepared to accept the sovereignty of the Islands in question—nor to rule them by a Protectorate government," wrote Peirce in his instructions to Meade in 1872.[35]

By 1883 an American policy had crystallized which came close to a spheres-of-interest arrangement—except in relation to Samoa, where the United States insisted on the preservation of American rights under the 1878 treaty. The American

---

[32] Ryden, *The Foreign Policy*, 78, 81, 137; *Cambridge History of the British Empire*, VII, pt. I, 353.

[33] *Ibid.*

[34] Scholefield, *The Pacific*, 153; Dunbabin, *The Making of Australasia*, 211.

[35] Quoted by Ryden, *The Foreign Policy*, 61.

attitude toward the distant outlying groups of Polynesia, the
State Department said, was different from that toward the
"intimately connected commonwealths of the Northern Pacific." The Australian agitation for annexation of such groups
as the New Hebrides, the Solomons, and adjacent islands
was not objectionable. Those islands were geographically re-
lated to Australia more than was Polynesia. They had been
developed largely by Australians and were not yet ripe for
self-government. So the United States was not concerned
over the strengthening of the ties between those islands and
the Australian colonies; neither the sympathies of the
American people nor their direct political or commercial relations were threatened by such a strengthening. Hawaii and
Samoa were exceptions deserving a different treatment, because by their form of government and their treaty relations
they had become independent members of the society of
nations.[36] In other words the United States government at
this time recognized that propinquity and colonizing activity
created certain rights of predominance—providing, apparently, that those rights did not interfere with the sympathies
or the political and commercial relations of the American
people.

In Australia this policy must have been welcome, although
at the time there was only mild anxiety over American interference with colonial interests (despite continued agitation
in America for annexation of Samoa after 1883)[37] because
the attention of Australians was almost completely absorbed
by French and German imperialism in the southern and
western Pacific. Especially during the years following 1883
the German moves toward annexation of Samoa and New
Guinea and the French plans to send convicts to the New
Hebrides caused excitement bordering on hysteria in the
Australian colonies and in New Zealand.[38] The colonists were
enraged by the refusal of the Colonial Office under Lord

[36] *U.S. For. Rel.*, 1883, 574ff.

[37] *Congressional Record*, xx, pt. 2:1285 (1889).

[38] See Victoria, *Parliamentary Debates*, XLVII:2114, 2269 (1884); XLVIII:83,
106ff (1885); LII:1096ff (1886); *London Times*, January 19, 24, February 25,
April 18, 21, May 6, July 15, 22, 1884.

Derby—"secure in his bed in a leading and well policed London square" and not easily to be disturbed in his equanimity "by merely epistolary and telegraphic groans from his antipodes"[39]—to inaugurate an aggressive Pacific policy. "The exasperation here is boundless," cabled the Victoria premier to London.[40]

Indicative of the feeling in Australia was a letter in the *London Times* signed by "Australasian," which suggested that Australians might go to war against France in the New Hebrides if recidivists kept coming. This could start a European war over mastery in the Pacific. If Great Britain would not help Australia, said the letter, the colonies might throw themselves into the arms of the United States, which might seize the opportunity of becoming a first-class naval power, and convert the whole Pacific into an American lake.[41]

Except for a few individuals, Americans had no such extreme ambitions, but "Australasian" correctly gauged the trend in American foreign policy. Difficulties among the natives and the three powers on Samoa, threatening to result in the exclusive domination of the islands by one power and thus to destroy their nominal independence, suddenly brought forth an unusually vigorous assertion of American rights. And the public support of the assertion indicated that Americans were no longer indifferent to happenings in that part of the Pacific. America now had a political anchor in the south Pacific, and was not satisfied with influence over the northern Pacific alone. The United States had definitely entered its age of imperialism—although as yet the main American policy was not to object to the annexation of islands but to insist on equal treatment for American citizens by the annexing power.[42] The pioneering work of the traders, the

[39] *London Times*, May 6, 1884.

[40] Victoria, *Parliamentary Debates*, xlviii:83 (1885); Dispatches, Melbourne, ix, October 1, 31, 1883.

[41] *London Times*, April 16, 18, 21, July 15, 22, 1884; Victoria, *Parliamentary Debates*, lii:1096 (1886).

[42] See John Bassett Moore, *Four Phases of American Development: Federalism, Democracy, Imperialism, Expansion* (Baltimore, 1912), 187f; and *A Digest of International Law* (Washington, 1906), i:423, 426; *U.S. For. Rel.*, 1892, 444; 1893, 566ff.

whalers, the missionaries, and the naval officers was showing results.

In educating the public to the importance of the whole Pacific and of the status of the U.S. in it, eager expansionists employed the usual arguments. First, reasons of security demanded the full assertion of American rights and interests in the Pacific everywhere. The United States, so the reasoning was, had a huge Pacific front faced by formidable European military and naval establishments in the Pacific westward and northward. The Asiatic empires were improving their art of war, threatening to become an additional danger to the United States. Aggressive and powerful Great Britain, especially, had a ring of forts around the United States, reaching from Hongkong, via Singapore, Sydney, and the Fijis, to Canada. This menace demanded an answer from America.[43] The United States had no control over the Pacific, but it should have.[44]

Second, economic reasons required a fuller participation of the United States in the affairs of the Pacific, even though trade with the South Sea Islands and Australasia might as yet be on a small scale. There was great rivalry among the powers for the carrying trade and commerce across the ocean, and in this the United States should participate. The importance of the Pacific Coast states and their future lay in the Pacific. Australia, New Zealand, and the islands were America's commercial neighbors, and the United States should not stand idly by while other nations were monopolizing the trade.[45]

These general reasons were applied specifically to the maintenance of America's position in Samoa. Others were added, such as considerations of national honor and the extension of the Monroe Doctrine to include that area of the

[43] *Congressional Record*, xix, pt. 1:258ff (1888). In Great Britain some analysts of the strategic situation in the Pacific came to the opposite conclusion. They considered Britain's position hopeless in the face of America's potential strategic position. "Naval Power in the Pacific," *Edinburgh Review*, clii:47 (1880).

[44] H. C. Taylor, "The Control of the Pacific," *Forum*, iii:411 (1887).

[45] *Congressional Record*, xix, pt. 1:265f (1888); xx, pt. 2:1332 (1889).

Pacific. A naval station on Samoa would be vital for the defense of the Pacific Coast, and for the sake of the promising trade with Australia, an American station in Samoa should be retained under all circumstances.[46] Indeed, the importance of Samoa for American-Australian commercial relations was one of the strongest arguments in favor of the American base at Pago Pago.[47]

The insistence of America upon the independence of the islands and the preservation of American rights there did not solve the difficulties created by the presence of three powers in the territory. The treaty of Berlin in 1889, reaffirming the neutrality and independence of Samoa and the equal status of the foreign powers, did not improve the situation. General dissatisfaction among all concerned continued.[48] The Australian colonies persistently voiced their criticism of British policy and complained that their interests were being sacrificed to British European interests.[49] In the United States a strong feeling existed, shared by President Cleveland, that the Samoan troubles were a just punishment for "entanglements" in faraway lands, but there was disagreement on the solution of the problem. A minority advocated complete withdrawal.[50] The majority was in favor of retaining American rights, but could give no advice as to how this could be done without prolonging the existing complications.

The problem was finally solved when the McKinley administration pursued a decidedly annexationist policy, and sup-

[46] *Ibid.*, xx, pt. 2:1325ff; George H. Bates, "Some Aspects of the Samoan Question," *Century Magazine*, xv (n.s.):945ff (1889).

[47] *The Nation*, XLVIII:84 (1889), doubted the sincerity of the argument in view of the fact that the tariff on wool had just been raised, hampering possible trade with Australia.

[48] Ryden, *The Foreign Policy*, 551ff.

[49] *U.S. For. Rel.*, 1888, 730f. During an Australasian convention in November 1883, a resolution was adopted of which the first clause read as follows: "That further acquisition of dominion in the Pacific south of the equator by any foreign power would be highly detrimental to the safety and well being of the British possessions in Austral-Asia, and injurious to the interests of the empire." *Melbourne Argus*, December 19, 1883. The American consul called this resolution "an enunciation of the Monroe Doctrine in its most pronounced form." Dispatches, Melbourne, IX, January 2, 1884.

[50] Callahan, *American Relations*, 145f.

ported the treaty of 1899 by which Samoa was partitioned between the United States and Germany. By that treaty Great Britain withdrew from Samoa, much to the chagrin of the Australian colonies. They knew they had been betrayed and their wishes sacrificed in favor of Britain's European and Near Eastern policy.[51] They accepted their fate with a "generally regretful acquiescence." In an article entitled "British Sacrifices for Teuton Friendship" the *British Australasian* praised the Australian colonies for the way in which they accepted the Samoan deal. This, the article said, was evidence of the colonies' responsibility in matters of broad imperial concern. The advantages Great Britain received in return for her retirement from Samoa and the guarantee of equal commercial treatment in the islands was some consolation to Australians, but the fact that the United States remained in Samoa did most to reconcile them to the new arrangement.[52]

[51] See *Die Grosse Politik der Europaeischen Kabinette* (Berlin, 1921–27), VIII:416ff; G. P. Gooch and H. W. V. Temperley, eds., *British Documents on the Origins of the World War, 1898–1914* (London, 1926–38), I:110, 122; "The New Pacific," *Littel's Living Age*, CCXXIII:262 (1899); John G. Leigh, "The Powers and Samoa," *The Fortnightly*, LXXI:55, 65 (1899); *U.S. For. Rel.*, 1888:730ff; E. Fitzmaurice, *Life of Granville* (London, 1905), II:431.

[52] XVII:1756 (November 16, 1899).

CHAPTER VII

The American-Australian
Far Eastern Triangle

THE approach of western imperialism to the shores of Australia produced a result of fundamental significance: federation of the colonies into the Commonwealth of Australia in 1900. There had been internal reasons for the unification of the colonies, and suggestions for federation had been made by individuals since the middle of the century. But the one force which succeeded in overcoming the dividing jealousies and in arousing popular support for federation was fear of aggression by foreign powers. Before the penetration of imperialist interests into the southern and western Pacific, the colonists saw "little to unite for, and nothing to unite against."[1] When the western nations established jurisdiction over the neighboring islands, union became a condition of survival to Australians.

American history and political institutions greatly influenced the federation movement and the constitutional form of the Commonwealth. The history of the development toward self-government in the individual colonies repeated itself: American precedents were a constant source of argument during the process of federation and the making of the constitution. They were not slavishly followed, but were adopted or rejected as Australian conditions seemed to require. Positively or negatively, the American federation left its mark on the Australian Commonwealth.[2]

The federation movement was accompanied and survived by the growth of a national feeling—also explainable as a reaction to the spread of imperialism—which in many cases quickly deteriorated into chauvinism and jingoism. Judging

[1] A. Wyatt Tilby, *Australasia, 1688–1911* (Boston, 1912), 208.
[2] Erling M. Hunt, *American Precedents in Australian Federation* (New York, 1930), is complete on this subject and nothing new can be added here.

81

by parliamentary speeches and large sections of the press, many Australians were seized with some extraordinary ideas about themselves, their part in the world, and the world in general. The danger to national security was magnified beyond reasonable proportions, giving Australian foreign affairs an unrealistic slant. Apprehensions which had disturbed the colonists for at least half a century—foreign aggression and the "yellow danger"—grew to gargantuan proportions and caused incongruous agitation and activities. Every issue in Australia's national life became somehow connected with defense and the "yellow danger," and was used for the stimulation of nationalism.

The outcome of this commotion about Australia's external relations was the demand for a share in running the affairs of the Pacific region and a strong self-assertion in all matters considered vital to the nation, even at the risk of diversion from British imperial policy.[3] The insistence of the *Melbourne Argus* in 1895 that "no treaty development in the Pacific should be allowed to take place without our claim to participation in it being advanced" was gaining official and widespread support.[4] This idea was implied, of course, in the well-established "sphere of interest" concept, but the broad claim to consultation was an expansion of the notion that affected primarily imperial relations—England was still taking care of Australian external relations—and indirectly Australia's contacts with other powers.

The focus of the immigration issue had always been Asiatic, but the target of the defense argument had changed nationalities frequently. After 1895 Americans, French, and Russians were finally replaced by Japanese. Thus, between 1895 and 1914, the major problems of Australian foreign relations (involving also the major issues of tariff and protection) pointed toward the Far East. Eventually the questions of defense, immigration, general foreign policy, and even social and labor policies melted into one and centered around Japan. Simultaneously and partly for the same reasons, Japan began to

[3] *Cambridge History of the British Empire*, vii, pt. i, 533.
[4] Quoted by *Japan Weekly Mail*, February 2, 1895, p. 144.

be the foremost preoccupation of other nations as well. The Far East turned into the world's main center of interest. As a consequence America and Australia came into touch through their Far Eastern policies more than through direct contacts.

Australia's Far Eastern policy was based on a mixture of rational and irrational elements: fear, mistrust, desire for friendship, quest for trade. Before Japan became a first-class power, Australian interests were directed toward China. Trade relations had been established at an early date and Chinese coolies had been brought to Australia before the middle of the nineteenth century. Sporadic opposition to this practice had been expressed then, but when the gold rush attracted large numbers of free immigrants, this opposition became general, leading to bad riots in the gold fields. The race problem quickly developed into a political issue. Clamor for the exclusion of Chinese immigrants endangered England's China policy and opened discussion of colonial interference with imperial policy, which, in turn, stimulated demands for colonial autonomy. The debate became more acrimonious when the problems of "cheap labor" were introduced.

As China increased its contacts with the outside world and gave signs of military prowess in the struggle with France, the specter of aggression appeared promptly in some Australian minds and the whole debate broadened to include defense and foreign policy generally. The result was animosity against Asiatic immigration, the passage of strict immigration laws, and a radical reduction in the number of Chinese in Australia. The Chinese question then moved into the background and was soon overshadowed by the Japanese question,[5] but it had served to crystallize most of the basic elements which have characterized Australian Far Eastern relations ever since. The changes in these relations after 1895 were mainly in their becoming more frantic, owing partly

[5] For details see Myra Willard, *History of the White Australia Policy* (Melbourne, 1923); I. Clunies Ross, ed., *Australia and the Far East* (Sydney, 1936), chap. i; Jack Shepherd, *Australia's Interests and Policies in the Far East,* (New York, 1940), chap. i.

to the greater aggressiveness of the Japanese, partly to the growing nationalistic spirit in Australia, and partly to the political changes in the Pacific.

Two events attracted Australian attention to Japan: the war with China, and the Anglo-Japanese treaty of 1894, which was open to participation by the self-governing colonies and which contained a clause permitting the signatories unrestricted immigration into each other's country.

At first the Sino-Japanese war was little noticed in Australia, while the Anglo-Japanese treaty awakened interest in things Japanese.[6] Japan's victory in the war came as a surprise to the colonies, though a pleasant one. Colonial sympathies were with the Japanese, and the colonies disapproved of the intention of some western powers to prevent Japan from obtaining a foothold on the Asiatic mainland as a fruit of victory. At the time Russia was the country that Australians feared as a potential aggressor.[7] The idea of a Russian warm water port within striking distance of Australia was intensely disliked, and the colonies felt that a Japanese base on the Liaotung Peninsula, for instance, might be an excellent check on Russian ambitions. The Australians thus were advocates of a balance of power policy between Japan and Russia years before this policy was adopted by Great Britain and the United States. The possibility that Japan might become a threat to Australian security did not immediately occur to the colonists; Japan was not considered a match for the combined Anglo-Australian forces. Only a very few Australians realized the implications of the Japanese victory, and their thoughts turned quickly to an alliance and trade.[8]

Australian public opinion soon changed, however. Under the leadership of colonial militarists, who capitalized on an unofficial statement by a Japanese that the good work in

---

[6] *Japan Weekly Mail*, October 13, 1894, p. 430; February 2, 1895, p. 144, April 20, 1895, p. 459. The last issue contains the first of a series of articles by John Plummer dealing with Australian-Japanese relations and providing an excellent survey of the Australian press.

[7] *Ibid.*, April 6, p. 409, June 29, p. 729, 1895.

[8] *Ibid.*, April 20, 1895, p. 459.

China should be continued in Hongkong, the Philippines, and Australia (an idea that was taken seriously in Australia only after it had been repeated often), Japan replaced Russia in the role of potential aggressor. Simultaneously, though, the prospect of increased trade with the new Japan proved very alluring to the colonial mercantile community.[9] Australian shippers of agricultural and dairy products had succeeded in making inroads upon America's Far Eastern trade, and the Anglo-Japanese treaty promised further stimulus to Australian-Japanese trade.[10] Torn between the lure of material gain and the fear of "yellow invasion" by either cheap labor, cheap goods, or armies, the colonists searched for a solution to this puzzling situation. Groups with concrete interests made their choice quickly, but others could not honestly decide between the dictates of their reason and their anxiety.[11] Eventually, influenced by the atmosphere of nationalism and foreign imperialism in the Pacific, the colonies, with the exception of Queensland, decided not to partake in the Anglo-Japanese treaty.[12] The "White Australia" policy, dormant since the expulsion of the Chinese, became a prominent issue once again.

A peculiar type of racism swept the colonies and the racist argument was introduced into almost every issue. Often it confused Australian thinking on foreign affairs. A typical example may indicate how unrealistic some ideas were. "The manifest destiny of Australia," Queensland Attorney-General Byrnes said, "is to be a country for the Anglo-Celtic race. We are to be dominant in the Southern Pacific. We may yet want a voice in the Northern Pacific as far as Honolulu is concerned if it is to be made a Japanese colony."[13] Sometimes racial discrimination was severely criticized in

[9] *Ibid.*, April 20, p. 459, April 27, p. 492, June 15, p. 661, June 29, p. 729, 1895.

[10] *Ibid.*, September 29, 1894, p. 359; January 18, p. 78, February 15, p. 199, March 7, p. 280, April 11, p. 428, May 2, p. 513, 1896.

[11] *Ibid.*, January 4, p. 17, February 15, p. 199, March 7, p. 280, 1896.

[12] Australia, *Parliamentary Debates*, XLI : 5867ff; *Japan Weekly Mail*, May 16, 1896, p. 562.

[13] *Ibid.*, May 2, 1896, p. 513. On the Australian concept of race, see C. Hartley Grattan, *Introducing Australia* (New York, 1942), 188ff.

Australia, but in practice the people were united from then on upon the "White Australia" doctrine.

The American immigration policy in regard to Asiatics created the impression in Australia that the Far Eastern policy of the United States and the colonies rested on the same foundation. This was an exaggeration. Emphasis on the race question was much more general in Australia than in America. Besides, Americans were little afraid of a Japanese invasion; trade considerations influenced immigration policy more than in Australia; and the United States was not quite as "Anglo-Saxon-Celtic" as Australians liked to believe. Though Secretary of State Olney wrote to Joseph Chamberlain in 1896 that "because of our inborn and instinctive English sympathies, proclivities, modes of thought, and standards of right and wrong, nothing would more gratify the mass of the American people than to stand side by side and shoulder to shoulder with England in support of a great cause,"[14] he could not deny that half the Americans had no "inborn and instinctive English sympathies," and that this fact always had a considerable influence upon any American foreign policy. Another important factor ignored by the colonists was that America was independent in the shaping of its Far Eastern policy, whereas the colonies had to accommodate themselves, at least to a degree, to British Far Eastern policy.

Nevertheless, as soon as the colonists discovered the similar elements in their and America's Far Eastern policy, they naturally looked to the United States for support and American-British relations became of growing importance to them. English overtures for closer cooperation with the United States after 1895 were most welcome to the colonies, the more so as this cooperation was especially desired in the Far Eastern region.[15] Any increase of American interest in the Far East seemed a good thing to the colonists.

For these reasons Australian sympathies were entirely on

[14] Alfred L. P. Dennis, *Adventures in American Diplomacy, 1896–1906* (New York, 1928), 60.

[15] See A. Whitney Griswold, *The Far Eastern Policy of the United States* (New York, 1938), chap. ii.

the side of America in the Spanish-American war. Formerly Australians would have feared American possession of the Philippines as a new "menace," but in the atmosphere of Anglo-American rapprochement and blind preoccupation with the Japanese threat, American entry into the Philippines was greeted as a first and most important step toward Anglo-American cooperation in the Far East.[16] Indeed, there was great hope in the colonies that American policy might be closer than British policy to Australian aims, since warnings had come from England that Australia should not impede Oriental trade through racial prejudice![17]

Occasionally, someone found the courage to decry the Anglo-Saxon myth. One writer, pointing out the absurdity of the "kith and kin" argument, mentioned that during his trips through the American Middle West he found that nobody understood English. The Tower of Babel, he concluded, must have been razed in the middle of the United States, and the builders settled there.[18] But this was a lonely voice. Generally, there was a strong desire for an alliance or close understanding between England and America in all matters of foreign policy, and this was based largely on a vague sentiment of Anglo-Saxon affinity.[19]

The annexation of the Philippines was welcomed not only on general principle but also because it came just at a time when the mother country was in danger of losing its predominant position in China, when the threat of Japanese expansion was growing, and when conditions in China were very precarious. The possibility of Britain's getting involved in war was not ignored, and if this should happen the fight would really be for the future of the white race in the great southern colonies and the Pacific. Naturally, Australia would stand by England, and so would the "new Anglo-Saxon masters of the Philippines." In the inevitable struggle between the races, the United States, Great Britain, and Australia

---

[16] *British Australasian*, XVI:984 (May 12, 1898), XVI:1612 (August 25, 1898).
[17] *Japan Weekly Mail*, April 6, 1895, p. 409.
[18] *British Australasian*, XVI:1037 (May 19, 1898).
[19] *Ibid.*, XVI:984 (May 12, 1898).

would stand shoulder to shoulder.[20] Nothing could shake the conviction of Australians in this theory. For at least two decades, until the end of World War I, it remained their criterion for the evaluation and interpretation of American Far Eastern policy.

The conclusion of the Anglo-Japanese alliance in 1902 was almost as well received in Australia as it was by John Hay and many other Americans. For a moment there were doubts in Australia regarding England's wisdom in concluding an alliance with the nation against whose nationals the colonies were discriminating. However, when Australians realized that there need be no concession in their immigration policy but only a little more conciliatory treatment of the power which was now to protect them, they approved of the alliance and hoped the United States would join.[21] The "yellow danger" seemed banned, at least for the duration of the alliance, and the great Pacific powers could live in friendship together. Australians were content, although an undertone of caution and skepticism never entirely disappeared.

This contentment lasted beyond the renewal of the alliance in 1905. The implications of Japan's victory over Russia, though not ignored, were of little concern to the Australians. This was strange, since the somewhat less sensitive Americans, especially Theodore Roosevelt and his friends, became quite disturbed about the prospects of a Japanese attack upon the Philippines. The change of American feeling toward Japan after 1905, added to the effects of the discriminatory American immigration policy, substantially worsened American-Japanese relations; the American press was full of war talk. Only then did the Australians become alarmed. Under the terms of the 1905 Anglo-Japanese alliance, Great Britain could be drawn into a war on the side of Japan,[22] making the situation most uncomfortable for the Commonwealth. The only pleasant aspect of the situation to

[20] *Ibid.*, XVI : 1129 (June 2, 1898); XVI : 1612 (August 25, 1898).

[21] *Ibid.*, XX : 304 (February 20, 1902); *London Times*, February 14, 17, 1902; cf. Australia, *Parliamentary Debates*, XLIII : 8507.

[22] See Griswold, *Far Eastern Policy*, 122ff.

Australia was the fact that seemingly American immigration policy had now become identical with Australian policy and showed the same results, thus bringing America and Australia even closer in their relations with the Far East.

The true feelings and ideas in the Commonwealth became clear when the American fleet under Admiral Sperry visited Australia in 1908. The official announcement that the American government had accepted Australia's invitation to the fleet[23] was followed by speculation on the meaning of the fleet's voyage and discussion of the international situation in the Pacific generally. There was common agreement that to Australia the entry of the American fleet into the Pacific was "something more than a stately procession of ships."[24] The timing of the fleet's transfer from the Atlantic right after the anti-Japanese riots in California was duly noted, and the voyage was interpreted as an anti-Asiatic move. Statements to the effect that the American fleet had accepted the Australian invitation to demonstrate the solidarity of the white race in the Pacific, or that Australia saw in America "the standard-bearer in the Pacific of the white race; [saw] America, like herself, confronted by the danger of a mongol incursion" reflected current public opinion.[25]

This presumed community of interest and outlook was further strengthened by frequent references to the similar characteristics of the American and Australian peoples. Both, an English observer wrote, were characterized by "their self-confidence and buoyancy, their *newness*, their sharply defined and rather material views of life, and their highly developed vision of an organized commercial and identical democracy unknown to our more delicately shaded and conservative society."[26] Others pointed to the similarity in natural surroundings and early pioneering activity.[27] This simi-

[23] State Department, Case 8258/109/123/124/333/358/403/407/408.

[24] *Review of Reviews*, XXXVIII:344 (1908).

[25] *Ibid.*; *Living Age*, CCLIX:121 (1908); *British Australasian*, XXVIII:3 (August 20, 1908); XXVIII:4 (August 27, 1908); *Melbourne Age*, March 17, 1908.

[26] *Living Age*, CCLIX:121 (1908).

[27] Percival R. Cole, *The United States and Australia*, International Conciliation 28, suppl. (New York, 1910), *passim*.

larity, it was explained, led to mutual understanding. American magazines and novels were more widely read in Australia than were English ones; Australian politicians studied their problems in the light of American experiences; Australian students visited American colleges; and there was a general familiarity with American life in Australia. Some observers even maintained that Australians understood Americans better than Englishmen, that adherence to English traditions was purely superficial, and some others, for these reasons, expressed fear about the possible effects of the fleet's visit upon Australian-British relations. Australia might come to rely more upon the United States than upon the mother country. This idea, Prime Minister Deakin said, was "too silly for words," but a good many Australians held it nevertheless.[28]

In vain Admiral Sperry tried to counteract this sentimental approach and bring a more realistic touch to American-Australian relations by pointing out in his speeches that without a consolidation of material interests and the development of American and British territories in the Pacific mere blood ties would count for little. In an even franker conversation with the Australian prime minister he said that every dollar the two countries spent on the development of their trade in the Pacific islands was worth ten put into fortifications, "because the world would recognize the community of our commercial interests and would not dare affront us as long as we hold together."[29]

Some American press comments indicated the existence of similar feelings and ideas on the other side of the ocean. The *New York Times* wrote that in the future affairs in the Pacific could not be settled without a regard for Australia; that to an extent America's problems were identical with those of Australia. The *New York Herald* assured Australia that America would use its mighty power (against Japan) if need

---

[28] *London Times*, September 29, 1908; *British Australasian*, xxvii:3 (July 23, 1908).

[29] *London Times*, September 9, 23, 29, October 2, 1908; Letters of Admiral Charles S. Sperry, letters to his wife, September 9, 16, 1908.

be. The *New York Daily Tribune* expressed some concern over the possible Asiatic reactions to a "White America" and "White Australia" policy, but hoped that through their acts the white races would prove their supremacy.[30] When the fleet arrived in Sydney it received a tremendous welcome, more cordial, it was sourly remarked, than that received by the Prince of Wales when he came for the opening of the first Commonwealth parliament.[31] The numberless speeches of visitors and hosts were extremely cordial and equally meaningless, according to the custom on such occasions. Nevertheless, between the lines Australian satisfaction was evident at the restoration of the balance of power in the Pacific, which had been impaired by the withdrawal of the British fleet following the Anglo-Japanese alliance. Admiral Sperry called the fleet's visit a "monumental success."[32]

The comments of Australian statesmen and officials, after the fleet had gone, emphasized again that its visit was proof of the solidarity of the white race; the demonstration of cordiality between Australia and America would make a lasting impression upon the Asiatic peoples. Australia could no longer proceed on the principle "forgetful of the world and by the world forgot."[33] There was no doubt now in the Commonwealth that in a war between Japan and Great Britain America would be on the British side, so Australia would not have to choose between the United States or the mother country. Community of interest among all three nations, based on racial affinity, was assumed a priori in almost all discussions on the future of the Pacific. There was practically

[30] *London Times,* August 21, 1908; *New York Daily Tribune,* August 22, 1908.

[31] *Living Age,* CCLIX:120 (1908).

[32] *London Times,* August 24, 1908; *British Australasian,* XXVIII:5 (August 27, 1908). The contrast with the visit of the Japanese fleet two years earlier was remarkable. See *London Times,* April 26, May 10, 18, 22, 23, 28, 1906; Chassigneux, "L'Australie et l'Extrême Orient," *L'Asie Française,* VIII:261ff (1908); Admiral Sperry, letter to his wife, September 16, 1908.

[33] The fleet's presence was also used to urge the citizens to emulate America and build a large fleet of their own. Australia, *Parliamentary Debates,* XLVII:17, 26, 33, 47; *British Australasian,* XXVIII:4 (August 27, 1908); XXVIII:5 (September 3, 1908); George Houston Reid, "The American Fleet in Australia," *North American Review,* CLXXXIX:404 (1909).

no analysis of interests on more substantial bases—another indication of the emotional nature of Australian thinking in that period.

But by 1911 Australians were pushed back into the dilemma of trying to be on good terms with an England allied to Japan and an America hostile to Japan. There was divergence between American and British Far Eastern policies, and the Australian illusion of community of interests based on kinship and sentiment was destroyed. Great Britain too was in a dilemma, unwilling to antagonize either America or Japan, but an opportunity for a compromise appeared to offer itself. By changing the terms of the alliance so that neither party would have to go to war with a third power with which it had an arbitration treaty, and then by concluding such an arbitration treaty with the United States, Great Britain could remain at peace with both nations in any eventuality. The alliance was changed accordingly. However, the Senate did not ratify the arbitration treaty and England's position was not much improved, except that it had clearly indicated unwillingness to go to war with the United States,[84] and Australia had approved the renewal of the alliance in view of the anticipated situation.[85]

Australians had rationalized that the renewed alliance provided another breathing spell of ten years and that it was better to have Japan as an ally than as an assailant.[86] It did not escape them, however, that ten years provided a breathing spell for Japan also, and Japanese motives continued to be suspect in the Commonwealth. The Asiatic "menace" had helped arouse popular support for conscription and for the creation of an Australian navy by 1910.

As the world situation deteriorated toward 1914, fear of Japan again became the overriding preoccupation in Australia. No soothing speeches from London[87] could calm Australian minds. Criticism of the imperial defense scheme and

---

[84] Griswold, *Far Eastern Policy*, 166ff.   [85] *British Documents*, VIII:525.

[86] Australia, *Parliamentary Debates*, LX:62, 203, 389, 542; *London Times*, July 17, 1911; Ross, ed., *Australia and the Far East*, 27.

[87] Winston Churchill's speech in Commons on March 17, 1914.

doubts regarding the Anglo-Japanese alliance continued. The outstanding fact was that Japan was the dominant power in the Pacific and that Australia was ill secured against it.[38] The idea that Australia depended upon the Japanese fleet for protection was most repellent to the Australian statesmen and people.[39] Australia looked frankly to the United States for encouragement.[40] The feeling there was not unlike that in Australia. American Far Eastern policy was developing into something more than the mere protection of commercial interests. To the perennial tension over the race question was added anxiety over the fate of the Philippines and the possibility of Japanese ascendancy in the Pacific in conflict with similar American ambitions.

When World War I broke out, the United States became greatly concerned over the preservation of the status quo in the Pacific. The prospect of a Japanese occupation of the German islands seemed frightening. Bases there would offer an excellent opportunity for attack against the United States.[41] Australian and American policies became united in the attempt to prevent Japan from expanding into the Pacific under the pretext of assisting Great Britain.

This pressure from America and Australia raised a problem for Great Britain. The Anglo-Japanese alliance became a matter of "some embarrassment and even anxiety," for the British cabinet was aware that unlimited Japanese action in the Pacific was repugnant to Australia and could have a "disastrous" effect on American public opinion.[42] Great Britain had to restrain its ally, an unpleasant but essential task. Japan agreed to restrict itself to the Asiatic mainland and

[38] *Japan Weekly Chronicle*, April 30, 1914, p. 715; *Round Table*, IV: 393ff (1914); General Sir Ian Hamilton's speech on the Asiatic danger, *London Times*, May 14, 22, 1914; *Japan Weekly Chronicle*, May 28, pp. 873, 880, June 11, p. 973, June 18, p. 1002, 1914.

[39] *Ibid.*, May 21, 1914, p. 825; *Sydney Morning Herald*, May 20, 27, 1914.

[40] *Japan Weekly Chronicle*, April 30, 1914, p. 715.

[41] *Ibid.*, August 20, pp. 358, 361, 363, 374; August 27, p. 410, 1914; *Congressional Record*, LI, pt. 14: 13896, 14074 (1914).

[42] Viscount Grey of Fallodon, *Twenty-Five Years, 1892–1916* (New York, 1925), II: 103.

the China Sea.[43] Japanese activities, Count Okuma announced in a speech, would be limited to the elimination of
German influence from the Asiatic continent.[44]

Later, in the Diet, the government denied ever having
given any promises to that effect, and in October 1914 the
Japanese occupied Yap. Australia was alarmed and hastily
prepared an expeditionary force to occupy the remaining
German islands. But a note from London asked the Australians to confine their activity to the area south of the equator
and to leave the settlement of the island question to the peace
conference. Australia complied;[45] indeed, the Commonwealth
government went even farther. In 1917, when the British
government asked the Australian prime minister whether
there was any objection to a British pledge for support of
Japan's claim to continued control over the German islands
north of the equator after the war, Mr. Hughes answered
that his government offered no objection and would "carefully abstain from doing or saying anything likely to strain
or make difficult the relations between His Majesty's Government and Japan, either in regard to the future partition
of the Pacific or in regard to trade or any other matter."[46]
This reply was a blank check not signed by the Australian
people, and it caused bitter attacks against Mr. Hughes when
the affair became known after the war.[47]

All through the war Australians were apprehensive about
the future of the German islands and expected the worst from
Japan[48]—notwithstanding their gratitude for the convoying
activity of the Japanese navy.[49] America shared this uneasiness and Australia was therefore anxious to improve relations with the United States. Early in the war the idea of

[43] *Japan Weekly Chronicle*, August 20, p. 372; 27, pp. 407, 408, 411, 420,
1914; *New York Times*, December 30, 1916.

[44] *Japan Weekly Chronicle*, August 27, 1914, p. 407.

[45] *Cambridge History of the British Empire*, VII, pt. I, 574f.

[46] *Ibid.*, 575.

[47] Ross, *Australia and the Far East*, 30.

[48] *New York Times*, December 30, 1916, et al.

[49] William Morris Hughes, *The Splendid Adventure* (London, 1929), 33; *L'Asie
Française*, XVI : 50 (1916).

appointing a trade commissioner for the United States was discussed. This, it was pointed out in the Commonwealth parliament, could be useful for security reasons, for purposes of trade and financial assistance, and generally in view of the growing importance of America in the Pacific. Eventually, the United States might use Australia as a naval base! These arguments found general approval and in 1918 a commercial representative was sent to America. The event crowned an Australian policy designed to obtain the friendship of the United States.[50] When the peace conference opened, American-Australian relations were most cordial, but both governments had to realize that the similarity of their Pacific policies did not reach beyond the negative point of preventing Japan from obtaining the German islands.

[50] Australia, *Parliamentary Debates,* LXXVIII : 5475ff; LXXIX : 7818ff; LXXXII : 502, 902; LXXXIII : 2031; LXXXIV : 3351; *London Times,* August 11, 1917; *New York Times,* September 16, 1918. The neutrality of their American "cousins" early in the war was a great disappointment to Australians. See *New York Times,* January 16, 17 (sec. III), 22, 26, 27, 31 (sec. VII), February 7 (sec. VII), March 21 (sec. III), 1915.

CHAPTER VIII

The Paris Peace Conference

THE international situation in the Far East after the war was in the forefront of interest both in Australia and America, and the Far East continued to be the area in which the foreign policies of the two nations met most closely. The strengthened Japanese position in eastern Asia increased American and Australian animosity against their former ally. Great Britain with the other dominions, France, and Italy were not quite as fearful of Japanese ascendancy, were more conciliatory, and had definite commitments which tied them to Japan though they proved objectionable to America. Australia, sharing America's anti-Japanese feeling, could be expected to cooperate with the United States. Yet that unity which might have followed from so frequently quoted common interests and common antagonisms was lacking. There were two main reasons: First, in regard to the racial issues America pursued a contradictory policy,[1] whereas Australia was consistent; second, their policies differed in regard to security and the disposition of the German Pacific territories. Over these two problems the Australians waged their major battles with the Americans at the Paris peace conference.

The future of German colonies in general had been a frequent topic of discussion in Great Britain during the war period. The British cabinet had no desire to add further territories to the empire. A memorandum prepared in the Foreign Office in 1916 even envisaged the need for a transfer of territory to Germany if the war should end in a stalemate, and indicated no regrets in London on that account.[2] This attitude still prevailed when Lloyd George opened the imperial war cabinet in 1917. On that occasion he confined himself to expressing his hope that the colonial question

[1] Griswold, *Far Eastern Policy*, 249.

[2] David Lloyd George, *Memoirs of the Peace Conference* (New Haven, 1939), I:22.

would be dealt with as one of the problems in the general settlement of the war, not as the special problem of any particular dominion, and to stressing that, depending on the outcome of the war, some sacrifices might be necessary.[3] He was purposely brief on the colonial topic. Knowing the feelings of the dominions, he wanted to leave the question to unprejudiced discussion by the committees dealing with the peace plans.

The decision of the cabinet subcommittee on territorial problems was to transfer New Guinea and the Solomons to Australia. "This was," in Lloyd George's words, "the first occasion on which any indication was given that Britain meant as a condition of peace to retain its conquests in the German Colonial Empire. So far the British Government had formulated no such demand. It was mainly due to the insistence of the Dominion representatives." The imperial cabinet agreed that the British delegates to a peace conference should be guided by these proposals.[4] Even so, in Lloyd George's opinion, could peace have been bought at that moment by letting Germany keep those islands, no dominion would have insisted on annexation.[5]

When victory came to the Allies, Australia expected the Pacific islands to be taken away from Germany as a matter of course. New Guinea and other islands nearby were considered legitimate booty of the victors.[6] Australian views were well known in London, and were confirmed by a Commonwealth parliament resolution in July 1917 approving a declaration by Walter Long, the secretary of state for colonies, that no colonies should be left to Germany and that especially the return of the Pacific islands would be distasteful to Australia and a threat to peace.[7] Aware of Australian aims, Lloyd George informed Colonel House that he would be

[3] Lloyd George, *War Memoirs* (London, 1934), IV:1776.

[4] *Ibid.*, IV:1749. The secret agreement with Japan of February 16, 1917, came very close to a retention of German colonial territory.

[5] Lloyd George, *Peace Conference*, I:32.

[6] In 1883 Queensland had annexed Papua, but this annexation was not approved by London. Scholefield, *The Pacific*, 117ff.

[7] Australia, *Parliamentary Debates*, LXXVI:2367, 2371, 2382; LXXXII:292, 911, 1128, 1131. *New York Times*, November 19, 1918; *London Times*, August 15, 1917; Hansard, *Parliamentary Debates*, XCVII:1022 (1917).

confronted by a "revolution" in Australia if the islands were given back to Germany.[8]

In the spring of 1918 Australia's prime minister, William Morris Hughes, was on his way to London to participate in a meeting of the imperial war cabinet and, as it turned out, to become the Commonwealth's representative at the Paris peace conference. En route he stopped in the United States and initiated his fanatical campaign for Australia's Pacific island policy. He was received by President Wilson on May 29, and saw members of the cabinet and the congressional committees on foreign relations. He impressed upon them Australia's demand for the Pacific islands, not for the sake of empire but for security.[9] In a New York speech, after paying tribute to the friendly relations between his country and America during the war, he elaborated upon the German intentions of swallowing up the Australian continent. Such designs, he felt, must be frustrated forever. "This brings me to a matter of life and death importance to Australia. America, Australia, and New Zealand have common interests in the Pacific. And Australia looks to you, her elder brother, to stand by her around the peace table as well as on the field of battle. For if we are to continue to be a Commonwealth of free people, we must have guarantees against enemy aggression in the future. And this involves an Australasian Monroe Doctrine in the Southern Pacific."[10] The *London Times* and the *Daily Telegraph* approved of the idea, and felt that it must be of interest to all nations around the Pacific, especially the western United States, situated so much closer to the Far East than an ordinary map would indicate.[11] The editorials sounded like an invitation to America to adhere to such a "Monroe Doctrine," directed, obviously, against Japan.

[8] *U.S. For. Rel., Paris Peace Conference 1919*, I:407.

[9] *New York Times,* May 30, 1918; *London Times,* June 17, 1918; Lloyd George, *Peace Conference,* I:69.

[10] *New York Times,* June 1, 1918.

[11] *Ibid.,* June 5, 1918; *London Times,* June 3, 1918. Australian opinion on Hughes's "Monroe Doctrine" was divided; Labour members of parliament opposed it. Australia, *Parliamentary Debates,* LXXXV:5730, 5737, 5855, 6031, 6377.

In June 1918 Hughes left the United States, satisfied, he said, with the response in high American circles to his policy.[12] On his arrival in England he continued his crusade. Lavishly endowed with space in the press, he repeated his suggestion for an Australian Monroe Doctrine.[13] Throughout the summer and fall he freely gave interviews and made speeches. He was not troubled by inhibitions and never minced words. He showed himself to be an obstinate fighter for his ideas, uncompromising, convinced of Anglo-Saxon supremacy, and a "realist." "Not from the clouds of theory, nor the mists of visions, can the world hope for salvation" was his poetic reaction to the League of Nations, of whose feasibility he remained forever skeptical.[14]

At the secret meetings of the imperial war cabinet Hughes worked toward the same narrowly Australian goal with equal determination. He put Australia's case for the Pacific islands in the strongest terms.[15] In the preliminary intercabinet conversations on possible peace conditions, he had the satisfaction of obtaining agreement on the necessity of ceding New Guinea to Australia, Samoa to New Zealand, and Southwest Africa to the Union of South Africa, and that the mandate principle would not be applicable to these colonies.[16] The Monroe Doctrine idea did not get much support except from Sir Austen Chamberlain.[17] Other cabinet members could not so easily be got out of their "clouds" and "mists" into Mr. Hughes's clear atmosphere. He stubbornly kept hammering away at the danger of an easy peace for Germany and the Australian need for the Pacific islands. To make his point he attacked the planned structure of the armistice and the peace to follow. He began with a broadside against the Fourteen Points as a basis for the armistice, because they would remain the basis for the peace also and thus prevent the

[12] *New York Times,* June 17, 1918.
[13] *Ibid.*
[14] *London Times,* June 26, 1918; Hughes, *Splendid Adventure,* 84f; cf. *London Times,* January 10, 1919.
[15] Lloyd George, *Peace Conference,* I:75; Hughes, *Splendid Adventure,* 93.
[16] *Ibid.,* 83; Lloyd George, *Peace Conference,* I:342.
[17] *Ibid.,* I:122.

conference from demanding "what terms it thought just, right, and practicable."[18]

The empire should be careful, he continued, lest it find itself "dragged quite unnecessarily behind the wheels of President Wilson's chariot." America's war role did not entitle Wilson to be the "god in the machine at the peace settlement." American sacrifices were negligible, not even as big as Australia's. Lloyd George and Clemenceau "could settle the peace of the world as they like." America should receive the respect due to a great nation, but it was intolerable that Wilson should dictate how the world was to be governed. "If the saving of civilization had depended on the United States, it would have been in tears and chains to-day." Wilson's scheme was not practical at all. Wilson and his League were like a child and his toy; the child would not rest until it had the toy. Concluding, Hughes said that Wilson misunderstood two things about Australia: the nation's unity in its attitude toward Japan and in its position on the Pacific island question.[19]

When the Pacific islands were discussed a last time in the imperial cabinet before the delegates left for Paris, Hughes demanded a definite decision on the exclusion of New Guinea, Samoa, and Southwest Africa from the mandate system. Though the majority of the imperial cabinet opposed new territorial acquisitions by the empire and had acquiesced in the mandate system, they agreed to Hughes's request.[20]

This, then, was the position of the empire delegation at the opening of the peace conference. Hughes was the undisputed leader in this matter, and had the assistance of Massey, the prime minister of New Zealand, and General Smuts of South Africa. The remaining members of the delegation had originally not shared Hughes's opinions, but they opposed them much less determinedly than Hughes adhered to them; so he had succeeded in winning over a reluctant majority in the delegation.

---

[18] Hughes, *Splendid Adventure*, 93, 97.
[19] Lloyd George, *Peace Conference*, I:120ff.
[20] *Ibid.*, I:342; Hughes, *Splendid Adventure*, 100.

The official American plan for the disposition of German colonies had been vaguely announced in the fifth of the Fourteen Points: "A free, open-minded, and absolutely impartial adjustment of all colonial claims, based upon a strict observance of the principle that in determining all such questions of sovereignty the interests of the populations concerned must have equal weight with the equitable claims of the government whose title is to be determined." Unofficially, American ideas regarding the German colonies, and the Pacific islands in particular, were more concrete. Throughout the war sporadic references to the strategic value of the islands could be found in the press. Uneasiness about Japanese expansion into the Pacific never quite disappeared,[21] yet these apprehensions were neither sufficiently strong nor widespread enough to provoke popular demand for American annexation of any islands.[22] But the President and members of the State Department were concerned about Japanese progress in the Pacific. They realized the strategic importance of the former German Pacific islands for Guam, the major Pacific cable station, and for the line of communication between Hawaii and the Philippines. As a minimum, Wilson was anxious to keep the Japanese away from the islands.[23] He discussed the over-all policy of the problem involved with Lansing, and the secretary authorized a departmental study of the Pacific islands in all their aspects.

As a result of the conversations between the President and his advisers, the idea of American acquisition of the former German islands as war spoils was discarded as incompatible with the American war aim of "no material gains"; this did not, however, preclude the possibility of acquisition by some other means. Since the government was convinced of the desirability of establishing American control over the islands, the State Department continued its study of the Pacific islands with a view, first, toward establishing possible claims

---

[21] See George H. Blakeslee, "Japan's New Island Possessions in the Pacific," *Journal of International Relations*, XII: 187 (1921–22).

[22] *U.S. For. Rel., Paris Peace Conference 1919*, II: 514.

[23] Lloyd George, *Peace Conference*, I: 118; Griswold, *Far Eastern Policy*, 246.

of ownership over some less important and contested islands (e.g., Marcus, Johnson, Howland, Baker), and, second, toward finding means by which eventually the more important former German islands could be acquired.[24]

The outcome was a memorandum prepared by Breckenridge Long and submitted to the American peace mission in Paris. Long reached the following conclusions: The United States was not interested in the islands held by British forces, except Samoa, in which America had a "considerable" interest. For strategic reasons America had an interest in some of the guano islands surrounding Samoa. These should be transferred from Great Britain to the United States. The Japanese-occupied islands were of "great importance" to America because of their strategic situation in relation to Guam and the Philippines. The United States could not claim these islands directly since Japan and Great Britain would have equally rightful claims, so the United States should insist that the islands be returned to Germany. Once they were again in German possession, the United States should ask for them in lieu of German reparations. This, Long went on, could not "morally" be done while the conference was in session, and it would be difficult to explain to the American people why the islands should be returned to Germany; but, on the other hand, the possession of these islands by Great Britain or Japan would be a "constant menace to the United States and its dominant position in the Pacific."[25] Here was a suggestion for another step toward American domination over the Pacific, and again the idea was ahead of public opinion, but nevertheless indicated the trend of thinking in high American government circles.

The mandate principle, so eagerly sponsored by Wilson, was a good compromise between Long's scheme of eventual annexation by America and the real danger of annexation by a foreign power. In Wilson's mind mandates may have been the next best thing to American possession of the Pacific

---

[24] From an unpublished manuscript by Breckenridge Long, "Pacific Islands"; cf. Blakeslee, "Japan's New Island Possessions," 189.

[25] *U.S. For. Rel., Paris Peace Conference 1919*, II: 513ff.

islands, or he may truly have believed that they were the best solution for the United States and the world. As was to be expected, abroad Wilson's support of the mandate principle was not entirely ascribed to unselfish internationalism. Observers noted that, to say the least, the mandatory principle was a smaller evil for America than possession of the colonies by foreign powers.[26] Whatever may have been the President's thoughts, on his arrival in Europe he favored the transfer of the colonies to the League of Nations under administration by the small powers.[27]

Wilson's position was almost as well known as Hughes's, and a clash between the two could easily be foreseen. Lloyd George and Balfour, his foreign secretary, were anxious to avoid such an unfortunate event at the peace conference. Being themselves favorably inclined toward the mandate system, but aware of their obligation toward Australia, they tried to arrange a compromise. Before Wilson's arrival they prepared the field by informing the American representatives in London of the imperial cabinet's decision not to restore the colonies to Germany and to permit the dominions to keep those colonies which they had captured. The American officials were noncommittal and obviously unwilling to prejudge the President.[28]

Even the most insistent pleading of Australia's cause by Lloyd George and Balfour before Wilson in their first "business meeting" could not move the President. When they stressed security reasons, Wilson replied that every other nation had a case on that basis. When they quoted the secret 1917 agreement with Japan, Wilson was unwilling to recognize the validity of the treaty, adding that he was not even certain about Japan's becoming the mandatory of any Pacific islands. He regarded it his function, he said, to prevent

[26] *New York Times*, January 29, 31, 1919; *London Times*, January 30, February 3, 1919.

[27] Charles Seymour, ed., *The Intimate Papers of Colonel House* (Boston, 1926), IV: 293; William E. Rappard, *The Quest for Peace* (Cambridge, Mass., 1940), 96.

[28] Lloyd George, *Peace Conference*, I: 66ff; Hughes, *Splendid Adventure*, 93.

disagreeable things, such as Japan's retention of the Pacific islands.[29]

In these preliminary skirmishes neither Wilson nor Hughes budged from his position. To each, recognition of his own viewpoint seemed vital for the success of the peace conference and the making of a better world. The ingredients of a dramatic battle were here.

On January 24, 1919, the dominion prime ministers were introduced into the Council of Ten meeting to plead their cause regarding the German colonies. The council at once agreed unanimously not to return the colonies to Germany. Then Lloyd George, in accordance with the decision of the imperial war cabinet, discussed the alternatives for the disposition of the colonies. As far as German New Guinea was concerned, he concluded that it should be treated as a part of Australian territory, mainly because it was contiguous to Australian-administered Papua and two different administrations in New Guinea would be wasteful and inefficient.[30]

Mr. Hughes followed with an exposition of his position. Strategically the Pacific islands encompassed Australia like fortresses, he began. New Guinea was big and only eighty-two miles away from Australia. Southeast of New Guinea was a string of islands useful as bases for an attack upon Australia. Australia could not defend its huge coastline, and could never feel safe with a potential or actual enemy at its very doors. The islands were as necessary to Australia as water to a city. He was against internationalization because, as Lloyd George had remarked, it would lead to confusion of authority with neighboring areas administered by Australia. If a power above Australia should exercise directive control, this power would overshadow the Commonwealth. National policies were liable to change; today's friends might be tomorrow's enemies; and from that standpoint Australia would consider a mandatory in New Guinea as a potential enemy. Australia's security would threaten no one, but Australia would suffer from insecurity. Australia as a democratic

29 Lloyd George, *Peace Conference*, i:118.
30 *U.S. For. Rel., Paris Peace Conference 1919*, iii:718, 720.

power would guarantee the welfare of the natives. Australian security and the great war sacrifices entitled it to freedom from fear. This speech contained every essential argument in favor of Australia's claim to the islands, and Hughes's later speeches were merely variations on the theme.[31]

President Wilson's reply to Hughes was the story of the man who bought an inordinate amount of real estate. When a friend asked him when this process of acquisition would stop, he answered that he would not be satisfied so long as anyone owned any land adjacent to his own. This, Wilson said, was apparently the main difficulty in Hughes's mind. Wilson accused the Australian of lack of faith in the League. In the age of the League no nation could take any territory away from the mandatory because this would make that nation an outlaw, and against this outlaw all nations, America in the lead, would rise and take up arms for the protection of the mandatory. "Therefore, all danger of bad neighbors was past." The only question was whether a mandatory could be as useful as direct Australian administration. He thought it could, because if the League did not succeed, the whole world would be in chaos anyway. If a successful administration by the mandatory should lead to voluntary union with the mandate, he, Wilson, had no objection. As to who should be the mandatory in New Guinea, his mind was open, and he did not object to Australia's being it.[32]

In the two speeches by the American and Australian statesmen their different *Weltanschauung* stood out as in a relief. A reconciliation was obviously most difficult. Nevertheless the British delegates still tried to prevent further antagonism or, worse, a possible break. Lloyd George, though inclined to support Australia, was searching for a compromise. Lord Robert Cecil in conversations with Colonel House tended to agree that Australia should have the islands as mandates. Apparently, he was impressed by House's argument that eventually the mandate could be persuaded to attach itself voluntarily to the mandatory.[33]

[31] *Ibid.*, 720ff; 745ff.   [32] *Ibid.*, 742.
[33] Seymour. *Intimate Papers of Colonel House*, IV : 294, 296.

After these conversations with Cecil, House told the President that with the exception of Hughes all British and dominion representatives were in favor of the mandate system, and he doubted whether public opinion in Australia was backing Hughes.[34] But on this point Australian officials and the conservative press tried to leave no doubt. During the critical days at the end of January the Commonwealth government and the conservative newspapers fully supported Hughes. Watt, the acting prime minister, cabled to Paris strong objections against the mandate system, quoting the unanimously carried resolution "that the Senate and the House of Representatives of the Commonwealth of Australia declare it essential to the future safety and welfare of Australia that the captured German possessions in the Pacific occupied by Australian and New Zealand troops should not under any circumstances be restored to Germany, and that in the consideration and determination of proposals affecting the destination of those islands, Australia should be consulted."[35] Watt supplemented this resolution with the explanation that not for exploitation or aggrandizement but for safety the islands must come under British, Australian, or New Zealand control. He claimed to have the fullest popular support in this view. There were even threats of the serious effect upon empire relations should England refuse its backing to Australian demands. The islands, so vital for Australia, were no fit object for new fancy schemes of internationalization.

Yet there were sections of the Australian public who reasoned differently. The Labour press opposed annexation as incompatible with the war aims. Other newspapers warned against accepting the great burden mandates would represent, and were supported by many businessmen in this opinion. Even some of those who favored annexation did so only because of the uncertainty of the mandate system and because internationalization close to home—in Samoa and the New Hebrides—had appeared to be unsuccessful. In his

[34] *Ibid.*, 296.
[35] *New York Times*, November 16, 18, 1918; January 30, 1919.

stand against the League of Nations idea, Hughes was accused of grossly misrepresenting Australian public opinion.[86] In the face of this deadlock in the Council of Ten, Colonel House advised the President to resort to publicity; he should advertise Australia's standpoint and public opinion would force Hughes to give in.[87] Wilson did not follow this advice, but his adversaries did turn to publicity as a weapon. The French press, favoring Hughes, gave biased reports of the supposedly secret meetings, and Hughes himself granted interviews highly critical of Wilson.[88]

January 30 brought the clash. On the previous day General Smuts had drafted a compromise proposal on the mandate system upon which the British and dominion delegates had agreed (and which eventually formed the basis for the mandate clause, Article 22, in the League of Nations Covenant). Lloyd George introduced this draft proposal in the Council of Ten with the remark that the dominions had accepted it for the sake of harmony, not out of conviction. Mr. Hughes confirmed this, adding that grave interests, involving the fate of humanity, were at stake and he would therefore not oppose the views of President Wilson and Lloyd George beyond the point which would reasonably safeguard the interests of Australia. His colleagues in the Commonwealth cabinet were considering the details of the draft, and he would give his definite assent as soon as they had reached a decision.

President Wilson expressed gratification at the proposal, but thought that a final decision could not be reached until other facts, such as the details of the League of Nations organization, were known. This statement, Lloyd George retorted, filled him with despair. On such a basis no agreement could ever be reached, since one problem always depended

[86] *Ibid.; London Times,* January 29, 30, 1919; "An Australian View of Mr. Hughes in Paris," *New Statesman,* xiv : 399ff (1920); "Australia's Mandates," *New Statesman,* xvi : 724 (1920); *Round Table,* ix : 601ff, x : 179ff (1919); Australia, *Parliamentary Debates,* lxxxv : 5243, 5980, 5982, lxxxvi : 7782, 7784, 7796, 7801, 7947.

[87] Seymour, *Intimate Papers of Colonel House,* iv : 296.

[88] Ray Stannard Baker, *What Wilson Did at Paris* (New York, 1919), 31ff; and Wilson's complaints about the indiscretion of the press, *U.S. For. Rel., Paris Peace Conference 1919,* iii : 786f.

on the solution of a previous one. The dominions, he felt certain, would not agree with Mr. Wilson, and the proposal should be accepted provisionally at once. Mr. Hughes sided fully with Lloyd George. Wilson's statement, he said, disturbed the compromise, and his people at home would never accept such indefinite schemes as Mr. Wilson proposed.[39]

Wilson was much troubled by the pressure of the dominions—with French assistance—for an immediate settlement of the mandate question in principle and the assignment of the mandates to specific nations.[40] Apparently he became nervous and lost his temper during the afternoon session on that day, January 30. Mr. Massey of New Zealand, speaking on his own and Hughes's behalf, continued to urge immediate acceptance of the draft proposal. Mr. Wilson, in a dramatic speech, addressed himself to Hughes and Massey, asking whether he was to understand that Australia and New Zealand had presented an ultimatum to the conference. Was the draft proposal the maximum concession they were willing to make, and would they refuse participation in any agreement at all if the proposal were not accepted?[41] He pointed out how serious it was to defy world opinion, but even this appeal did not move Mr. Hughes from his position. "Mr. Hughes," Wilson said, "am I to understand that if the whole civilized world asks Australia to agree to a mandate in respect to these islands, Australia is prepared still to defy the appeal of the whole civilized world?" "That's about the size of it, President Wilson," replied Hughes.[42]

Late in the afternoon, after Wilson had accused Hughes of using threats, the Council of Ten accepted the draft proposal. This did not prevent Hughes from continuing his campaign against mandates.[43] In the course of his deprecations of the institution, he antagonized Wilson and other Americans by such statements as "Australia recognized the

39 *Ibid.*, 785ff.
40 Seymour, *Intimate Papers of Colonel House*, IV:297.
41 *U.S. For. Rel., Paris Peace Conference 1919*, III:799ff.
42 Lloyd George, *Peace Conference*, I:360.
43 *New York Times*, February 3, 9, 1919.

great cause immediately, not at the eleventh hour,"[44] and the Japanese by stating that mandates would permit the Japanese to overrun the islands close to Australia—a most undesirable prospect.

This remark caused a considerable stir in the Japanese Diet and press. The Japanese had stood with Hughes in his fight against the mandate system. Annexation of the islands had been accepted as a matter of course in Japan, but the Japanese were more conciliatory than Hughes and had remained in the background during the debate, letting the Australian take the onus of opposition. When Hughes attacked them, they accused him of ingratitude for war services rendered, and pointed out that Australia's move north was just as threatening to them as their move south appeared to be to Australia.[45]

On February 8 the Smuts proposal for the mandates was accepted almost without alterations by the League of Nations commission. For Australian (and New Zealand and South African) purposes the class C mandate was created through Section Six of Article 22 in the League Covenant: "There are territories, such as Southwest Africa and certain of the South Pacific islands, which, owing to the sparseness of their population or their small size, or their remoteness from the centers of civilization, or their geographical contiguity to the territory of the Mandatory, and other circumstances, can be best administered under the laws of the Mandatory as integral portions of its territory, subject to the safeguards above mentioned in the interests of the indigenous population."

This arrangement gave President Wilson the satisfaction of avoiding outright annexation, of having the mandate principle applied to all territories, and of having delayed assignment of mandates to individual nations until the League of Nations was established. Mr. Hughes and his col-

[44] *Le Matin*, February 3, 1919; *Japan Weekly Chronicle*, February 13, 1919, p. 259.

[45] *New York Times*, February 2, 1919 (sec. i); *Japan Weekly Chronicle*, February 6, 1919, pp. 182, 200; February 13, 1919, pp. 226, 243, 259.

leagues, Massey and Smuts, were happy in the knowledge that the C mandates were in reality nothing but disguised annexations and that the final assignment of mandates would coincide with the prior claims put forward by the occupying powers. Mr. Hughes made no bones about his interpretation of C mandates. Australians must have a "good frontier," he said; the islands must be theirs or so nearly theirs "that the difference between a leasehold and a freehold tenure would be a matter over which lawyers and metaphysicians could spend hours in profitless discussion."[46] On May 7, 1919, the islands south of the equator, with the exception of Samoa and Nauru, were definitely assigned to Australia as C mandates.[47]

Hardly had the battle over the mandates calmed down when new complications arose. The Japanese introduced an amendment to the Covenant recognizing the principle of racial equality. As was to be expected, the Australian representative was even more adamant in his objection to this scheme than to the mandate question. This was a point, he said, on which he could not give way and he might just as well speak plainly, which he did, as usual.[48] In this case his task was eased by more assistance from Balfour and Cecil.

The Japanese had broached the subject first with Colonel House. He visualized immediately the complications that would arise from the race equality idea, and drew up a number of different clauses in the hope of making the amendment palatable to Hughes.[49] The effort was in vain. Hughes insisted that nothing on this subject, "no matter how mild and inoffensive," should go into the Covenant. He threatened to stir up trouble in the plenary session and to arouse a storm of protest in the dominions and on the American West Coast if anything were attempted.[50]

For one fleeting moment Hughes seems to have been pre-

[46] *London Times*, April 26, 1919.   [47] *Ibid.*, May 8, 1919.

[48] *New York Times*, March 28, 1919.

[49] Stephen Bonsal, *Unfinished Business* (New York, 1944), 32; Seymour, *Intimate Papers of Colonel House*, IV: 308ff.

[50] *Ibid.*, 415.

pared for a compromise. The Japanese amendment would be acceptable to him if it specified that immigration remained a matter within the jurisdiction of each nation. When the Japanese proposed to settle this particular question by a gentlemen's agreement, Hughes returned to his original stand and cut off all further negotiations.[51] He had few sympathizers; the overwhelming majority of the delegates were against him.[52] Yet when the vote was taken, the empire representatives sided with him against the amendment; they were all "good Indians," according to General Smuts.[53] Nevertheless, with France, Italy, and the United States favoring the amendment (although Elihu Root had warned House that they would not get the clause through the United States Senate), the vote was almost two to one for the amendment. But Wilson ruled it "not carried" in view of the powerful opposition.[54] Hughes had scored another victory, this time possibly not to the entire dislike of Wilson, with the West Coast in mind.[55]

The encounter between the American president and the Australian prime minister was a clash between what each considered the vital interests of his country. It was also a clash between personalities, which embittered the debate. Neither statesman accurately represented public opinion at home. Wilson was somewhat more sanguine about the good new world than most Americans; Hughes was more pessimistic than many of his countrymen. In other words, public opinion in both countries would have permitted a more conciliatory way of reaching an agreement on the islands than the two statesmen had chosen. This may be why the friction between the American and Australian representatives at Paris had no lasting effect upon the relations between the two nations.

[51] "An Australian View of Mr. Hughes in Paris," 400.
[52] Hughes, *Splendid Adventure*, 107.
[53] Bonsal, *Unfinished Business*, 170.
[54] *Ibid.*, 154; Griswold, *Far Eastern Policy*, 249ff; cf. H. W. V. Temperley, ed., *A History of the Peace Conference* (London, 1924), vi:352ff.
[55] Griswold, *Far Eastern Policy*, 250ff.

CHAPTER IX

The Settlement of Pacific Problems

THE end of the war and the readjustment of Pacific affairs brought a number of misunderstandings between the United States and Australia. Their policies regarding the German colonies, and to a lesser degree the race issue, were the sources of the most important ones. But some other factors prevented sections of the Australian public from being wholeheartedly sympathetic to America. The disappointment over America's neutrality in the first war years, America's abstention from the League of Nations, and the refusal to cancel Allied war debts caused resentment in Australia.[1] However, this feeling never went very deep—except in the hearts of some ultranationalists—and did not halt the process of Americanization which had been going on since prewar days. American products, novels, magazines, songs, dances, fashions, films, "sures," and "gees" continued to invade the continent. The tide of enthusiasm for America and things American which started with the fleet visit in 1908 never quite ebbed, according to the *Sydney Morning Herald*.[2] Clearly there was a sentimental predisposition to cooperate with the United States and an awareness that both nations had some fundamental interests and antagonisms in common. Yet there were differences in point of view on the urgency and importance of individual problems and on their solution which even the greatest desire for friendly collaboration could not always overcome.

Australians realized dimly that the new status within the empire, acquired at Versailles and Geneva, burdened the nation with the task of policy-making and therefore with re-

[1] *Literary Digest,* LXXV:21 (November 25, 1922).

[2] *Ibid.; ibid.,* LXVI:21 (September 18, 1920); LXXVII:28 (May 12, 1923), 35 (April 7, 1923); Sydney Greenbie, "The Pacific Triangle," *North American Review,* CCXI:340ff (1920).

sponsibility. Membership in the empire now offered cooperation rather than shelter.[3] Australia's new role required initiative and closer contacts with nations bordering the Pacific.
The Australian desire for friendship with the United States
was wise from the standpoint of *Realpolitik,* but it was also
true that many Australians had a "very warm corner" in
their heart for America.[4]

In view of these postwar developments it was not surprising to hear for the first time mention of more than purely
commercial Australian representation in the United States.
However, Australian thinking had not yet caught up with
the newly acquired status and separate diplomatic representation looked too much like separatism to many Australians.
After much debate the Commonwealth government decided
upon a compromise. A commissioner was appointed who was,
as he himself emphasized, to advise his government on trade
but had in addition the general task of creating a "friendly
interest" for Australia in the United States. The idea of
diplomatic representation was not reconsidered until 1928,
when it was again discarded. For the time being Australia
was satisfied with having its foreign affairs run via London.[5]

The Commonwealth was greatly disturbed by a growing
tension between America and Japan, with the resulting arma-
ments race, just at a time when Great Britain and Australia
were suffering from the aftermath of the war. The air was
full of war talk, and the prospect of having to compete with
wealthy Pacific rivals or of being dragged into a war between
the two main competitors was grim. Friendship with the
United States and Japan and cordial relations among Pacific
powers were the goals of Australian policy. Success depended
upon the solution of the major problems in the Pacific: the
Anglo-Japanese alliance, disarmament, and Japan in China.
These problems became inextricably interwoven in the next

---

[3] *Round Table,* xii:184 (1921).

[4] Hughes in the *New York Times,* June 22, 1921.

[5] Australia, *Parliamentary Debates,* xciv:5539, 5605, 6730, 7250, 9377, 11819;
cxviii:7055; *London Times,* April 11, May 10, 1923; May 16, June 27, August
25, 1924.

few years over the question of renewing the Anglo-Japanese alliance.

America disliked the alliance. As soon as Anglo-Japanese conversations on a renewal of the alliance took concrete form, the State Department explained its position to London. If the alliance was to be renewed, the Foreign Office was informed, it should be very explicit, first, on the open-door principle in China and the maintenance of China's territorial and administrative integrity, and, second, on the fact that it was not directed against the United States.[6] The British government promised to heed these suggestions.[7] Furthermore, both parties to the alliance agreed to make it conform with the Covenant of the League, and in addition both repeatedly indicated that the alliance even in the existing form was not aimed at the United States.[8]

The American government was not satisfied with these assurances. In fact, it did not want to be satisfied because it was not overly worried about the possibility of British participation on the side of its ally in a Japanese-American war. Washington's real concern was over the support the alliance gave to Japan's Far Eastern policy, and the final American aim was to get rid of the alliance. The question of whom the alliance was directed against was discussed mainly to provide the opening for a mild attack upon the existence of the alliance altogether. This was made clear to the British government at an early stage in the conversations, and America's feelings against the alliance soon became common knowledge throughout the world.[9]

America's arguments against the alliance were these: American-British interests in the open-door principle and China's integrity could not be safeguarded by a common policy as long as Britain was prevented from freely joining in American protests against Japanese violations of those interests; Japan was using more than geographic proximity

[6] U.S. For. Rel., 1920, II, 679ff.   [7] Ibid., 682.

[8] Ibid., 685; Griswold, Far Eastern Policy, 278ff.

[9] For details on Anglo-American relations regarding the Anglo-Japanese alliance see Griswold, Far Eastern Policy, 274ff.

in gaining advantages in China, and renewal of the alliance would be interpreted as tacit British approval of this policy; protection against Russian and German imperialism, the original reason for the alliance, was no longer needed; some dominions shared America's feelings on the alliance.[10]

The British recognized the validity of some of these arguments and were most decidedly anxious to retain American friendship. But they also had reasons for continuing the alliance: the alliance had once been useful and Japan could not just be dropped; some dominions desired continuation of the alliance; Japan was a bulwark against the spread of Russian Communism; Japanese imperialism was easier to control with Japan as a friend than as an enemy.[11]

Japanese feelings on the renewal were mixed. Part of the press favored it; part opposed it. The government was in favor of renewal, but realized that American pressure upon Great Britain, increased by Canadian dislike of the alliance, might prove too strong. Tokyo therefore was resigned to the idea that the alliance might have to be changed substantially or might not be renewed at all.[12]

The Australian people, feeling that of all the "white" nations they were the most vitally concerned in Pacific affairs, took a great interest in this complex situation. In working out their policy the Australian people and many Australian statesmen misjudged the basic motive of American policy in the Far East. Blinded by their preoccupation with security and with the "white Australia" policy, they could see no other driving force in American policy. They realized that American security was not as immediately threatened as their own, so they believed the race issue to be the determinant in America's policy. Very few people in Australia were aware that the American-Japanese conflict arose primarily from a clash of interests in the Far East. The Chinese situation was neglected by Australians; some even thought

10 *U.S. For. Rel.*, 1921, II, 314ff; 1922, I, 1; *London Times*, June 18, July 9, 1921.
11 *U.S. For. Rel.*, 1920, I, 532; 1922, I, 1; Hughes, *Splendid Adventure*, 119.
12 K. K. Kawakami, *Japan's Pacific Policy* (New York, 1922), 47.

that the best solution of the Far Eastern problem would be to give Japan a free hand in China.[13] Therefore the major issue in the alliance situation appeared to Australians to be the ostensible one of whether Britain would be on Japan's side in case of war. It did not occur to them that this was a secondary consideration in Washington.

Australia's way through this maze of conflicting interests was—from the Australian viewpoint and interpretation— fairly clear. Prime Minister Hughes outlined it in the Commonwealth parliament in the spring of 1921. In view of the naval rivalry in the Pacific, he explained, there was great need for understanding among the English-speaking peoples and a renewal of the Anglo-Japanese alliance. These understandings might bring about a *détente* in the Pacific. "For this is the dilemma in which we are placed. While making every effort to retain the friendship of Japan we cannot make an enemy of the United States of America." It was their "bounden duty," Hughes continued, to effect a *modus vivendi* which would secure renewal of the alliance in a manner acceptable to the United States. His conclusion was that the alliance should be renewed under two conditions: one, the "white Australia" policy should not be endangered; two, any arrangement must be absolutely satisfactory to the United States.[14] The problem was a difficult one, and opinion in the Australian parliament was divided. Some members suggested an Anglo-Japanese-American alliance, which would have been welcome to many Australians,[15] but most members realized that this ideal solution was out of the question. The dilemma had to be solved in another way.

The Labour party was not subscribing enthusiastically to Hughes's views. After the prime minister's speech Labour members were silent. On the whole the party seemed inclined

[13] *New York Times*, April 12, 1921; *Japan Weekly Chronicle*, June 9, 1921, p. 807; F. W. Eggleston, "Washington and After, an Australian View," *Nineteenth Century*, XCII:459 (1922); *Conference of the Prime Ministers and Representatives of the United Kingdom, the Dominions, and India*, Cmd. 1474 (1921), 20.

[14] Australia, *Parliamentary Debates*, XCV:7262; *London Times*, April 8, 1921; *New York Times*, April 12, 1921; Hughes, *Splendid Adventure*, 119.

[15] Australia, *Parliamentary Debates*, LXXXIX:12398, 12403; XCVI:9383.

to sacrifice the alliance in favor of unimpaired friendship with
the United States. Not being quite sure of itself or of popular
opinion on the problem, the party demanded a referendum
but was defeated in parliament. Majority opinion was behind Hughes in favor of the alliance, reasoning that Japan
was more desirable as an ally than as an enemy.[16] Hughes,
determined to fight for continuation of the alliance, once
more went to England to participate in the imperial conference which opened June 20, 1921.

The renewal of the alliance quickly became the most hot-
ly debated issue at the conference. There was general agreement on the absolute necessity of nursing friendship with
the United States. (In fact, cordial sentiment in Australia
was growing so rapidly that suggestions of an American-
Australian "understanding" became exceedingly popular—
and some puzzled observers were questioning the mysterious
rise of such enthusiasm.)[17] But in spite of this great friendliness toward America, only Canada was willing to give up the
alliance. Hughes was its foremost defender, and he presented
his viewpoint essentially as he had done at home. There
should be disarmament and a renewal of the alliance with
the *conditio sine qua non* that war with America be specifically excluded. Furthermore, he added, the British government should find out what else America objected to in the
alliance and adjust it accordingly.[18]

Massey of New Zealand supported Hughes. Smuts favored
a compromise solution. Meighen of Canada remained adamantly opposed to the alliance. For days the discussion dealt
with the reconciliation of the Anglo-Japanese alliance with
friendship toward America and China.[19] Finally, Meighen
proposed calling a conference for the solution of Pacific

[16] *Sydney Morning Herald,* April 8, 12, 1921; *London Times,* April 8, June
23, 1921; *New York Times,* April 19, 23, 1921; *Japan Weekly Chronicle,* June
9, 1921, p. 807; cf. *Round Table,* xi:685 (1921).

[17] *London Times,* June 20, 1921; *Japan Weekly Chronicle,* December 29,
1921, p. 937.

[18] *Conference of the Prime Ministers,* 19ff; *London Times,* June 22, 1921; *New
York Times,* June 22, 1921; Hughes, *Splendid Adventure,* 120.

[19] *Ibid.,* 123.

problems, which might eliminate the need for the alliance.[20] This raised another problem, though. Such a conference could not be called without lengthy preparation; and it became a matter of controversy whether or not the alliance should continue in force during this interval. Eventually it was decided that a Pacific conference should be called, but that the alliance was not to be renounced until either the conference had been concluded successfully or a substitute treaty had been signed. While these conversations were going on, the Washington Disarmament Conference was called, and replaced the suggested Pacific conference.[21]

All empire members welcomed the Washington Conference. Each hoped that it not only might settle the manifold world problems but might also contribute to the solution of local difficulties. Australia, it was understood, was willing to let Great Britain handle the disarmament aspect of the Washington Conference alone, but was most anxious for a part in the discussions of Pacific problems.[22]

Hughes and his colleague Massey pressed the American ambassador in London for a meeting of the conference on Pacific problems before the disarmament conference and at such a time and place that they could participate. (Both prime ministers had to be home by October for the opening of their respective parliaments.)[23] In view of the extraordinary importance of the Pacific problems to be discussed, Hughes felt that no one but himself should speak for Australia.[24] However, the American government refused for several reasons to hold any conference preliminary to the main

[20] He had suggested this idea once before to Lloyd George. J. B. Brebner, "Canada, the Anglo-Japanese Alliance and the Washington Conference," *Political Science Quarterly*, L:53 (1935).

[21] Hughes states that agreement on Meighen's proposal was reached after the disarmament conference was announced; Griswold states it was reached before the announcement. Hughes, *Splendid Adventure*, 126; Griswold, *Far Eastern Policy*, 288.

[22] Hughes, *Splendid Adventure*, 131; *New York Times*, July 20, 1921; cf. *ibid.*, June 17, July 8, 1921.

[23] *U.S. For. Rel.*, 1921, I, 26; *New York Times*, July 22, 23, 1921.

[24] *U.S. For. Rel.*, 1921, I, 64; *London Times*, July 12, 1921; *New York Times*, July 21, 1921.

conference at Washington,[25] and this led to what was apparently a misunderstanding on the part of Hughes. He announced in the Commonwealth parliament that the dominions had attempted to secure separate representation at the Washington Conference but had given up after the United States "slammed the door."[26] Hughes interpreted America's refusal to hold a preliminary conference as a refusal to deal with the dominions directly.[27]

The facts of the matter were exactly opposite to what Hughes thought. The new status which the dominions had acquired at the Paris peace conference and in the League of Nations was informal as yet; Washington considered the dominions as component parts of the empire and did not deal with them as individual units.[28] Certainly in the case of Australia this was a proper procedure since the Commonwealth itself was satisfied with having its political relations taken care of by the British ambassador.[29] However, the problem had been recognized by the State Department as a delicate one, and Harvey, the American ambassador in London, took great pains not to insult either Great Britain or the dominions. Secretary of State Hughes was willing to accommodate the Australian and New Zealand prime ministers regarding the date of the Washington Conference, and was anxious to have the dominions represented. He informed Harvey that the presence of dominion delegates "would be very acceptable to the United States." He suggested five or six delegates for each nation so as to give Great Britain full opportunity to include dominion representation, "which the United States does not desire to make difficult."

However, the question of dominion representation did not arise in the conversations between Harvey and the Foreign Office because it was Harvey's impression that the British

[25] *U.S. For. Rel.*, 1921, i, 28, 37, 46, 49.

[26] Australia, *Parliamentary Debates*, xcvii:11716, 11729, 11735, 11738, 11763; cf. 11691, 11711.

[27] *New York Times*, October 8, 1921.

[28] *Ibid.*, July 23, September 29, October 8, 1921.

[29] *London Times*, August 22, 1922; April 11, 1923; June 27, 1924. Australia had only a commissioner in New York, who was not a diplomatic representative.

considered this a family affair. "In fact, they are so sensitive upon this point," he reported, "that I feel sure Curzon would have been disposed to resent any suggestion from me along this line." Besides, the ambassador felt, Curzon and Lloyd George did not want to have the dominion prime ministers participate in the conference on the same plane of authority with them. Harvey, however, expressly mentioned six delegates in his report to the State Department, so as to prevent any subsequent accusations that the United States was opposed to dominion representation.[30]

Senator Pearce was appointed as the Australian delegate. The public was intensely interested in the conference and aware of its importance for the future of the Commonwealth,[31] but Australian influence was only indirect. The big three— Great Britain, the United States, and Japan—conducted most of the business, and the burden of finding a solution to the Pacific problems acceptable to the empire fell upon Balfour. He was tied, of course, to the imperial conference agreement of either finding a substitute for the Anglo-Japanese alliance or admitting its continued existence. If the alliance was renewed in its present form, he would incur the wrath of the United States, Canada, and China; if he should break the imperial conference agreement and give up the alliance without a proper substitute, he would have to fight it out with Australia and New Zealand and antagonize Japan. Secretary of State Hughes proved to be the *deus ex machina* by producing the Four Power Treaty, which was eventually signed by Great Britain, the United States, France, and Japan on December 13, 1921.

This treaty pledged the mutual respect of the signatories for their insular possessions and insular dominions in the Pacific. In case of a controversy concerning rights in such

[30] *U.S. For. Rel.,* 1921, I, 39, 61, 64, 66, 72. The correspondence between the secretary of state and Harvey should prove that the United States government had no desire to exclude the dominions from the conference, yet Fred Alexander, *Australia and the United States* (Boston, 1941), 22, still states that "the United States Government did not at first contemplate Australian or other dominion representation at the conference."

[31] *New York Times,* September 22, 1921.

possessions or dominions, the signatories obliged themselves, failing diplomatic settlement, to submit the subject to all signatories for consideration and adjustment. In case of aggressive action by any power, the signatories agreed to discuss counter measures. The signatories finally agreed that the Four Power Treaty replaced the Anglo-Japanese alliance, and the empire accepted the treaty as a satisfactory sarcophagus for the alliance.

The other treaties concluded at the Washington Conference satisfied the Australian people. They seemed to inaugurate the era of collective security from which Australians expected the banishment of their perennial nightmare: foreign invasion of the continent. Some of the more pessimistic Australians, however, expected nothing more than another breathing spell permitting their country to become strong. The career of the United States was constantly before their minds, that nation in which they saw what they themselves hoped to be someday.[32] Increased immigration and increased industrial development would bring them closer to their ideal. If only Australia could be strong, all Pacific problems would be solved![33]

Among the explanatory agreements attached to the Four Power Treaty was one on which the United States insisted. It was a declaration that "the Treaty shall apply to the Mandated Islands in the Pacific Ocean; provided, however, that the making of the Treaty shall not be deemed to be an assent on the part of the United States of America to the mandates and shall not preclude agreements between the United States of America and the Mandatory Powers respectively in relation to the mandated islands."[34]

The reason for this declaration dated back several years. The American government was dissatisfied with the man-

[32] Hughes at the imperial conference, *New York Times,* June 22, 1921.

[33] E.g., Meredith Atkinson, "The Washington Conference. Australia's Position," *Nineteenth Century,* xc:941ff (1921).

[34] Text of Washington agreements in *Conference on the Limitation of Armament,* Senate Document No. 126, 67th Cong., 2nd Sess., 1922, 871ff; cf. Australia, Parliamentary Papers LXI No. 2, *Conference on the Limitation of Armament, Report of the Australian Delegate.*

date arrangements in general and in particular with the transfer to Japan of Yap, which was important for American strategy and cable communications. Secretary of State Hughes summed up the American position when he discussed the relation between the Four Power Treaty and the mandates: "We are not in the League; the League has granted a mandate to various powers for various territories; we did not agree to the allocation; we do not now recognize these mandates; we desire no territory for ourselves, nor do we wish to change the allocation of the mandates; we wish simply the same rights as others in these territories, and to be protected against discrimination by appropriate conventions."[85] In other words, the United States demanded the open door in the mandates. The open door was guaranteed only for the B mandates; Article 22 of the Covenant obliged the B mandatory to "secure equal opportunities for the trade and commerce of other Members of the League." There was no such stipulation for the C mandates; they were to be "administered under the laws of the Mandatory as integral portions of its territory."

Wilson had agreed to these terms of the mandates in the expectation that the United States would join the League and could request the open door in the B mandates. But a claim for the open door in the C mandates had only the flimsiest foundation, if any at all.[86] Nevertheless, the American government made a valiant attempt to recover the ground Wilson had lost. Early in 1921 the United States government raised the issue (for the second time) in regard to all mandates by sending a note to the League of Nations and Great Britain reserving the right to participate in the allocation and arrangement of mandates.[87] Great Britain, in a more conciliatory mood than the League, began a correspondence with Washington, strictly separating the various types of mandates and asking exactly what were American criticisms

---

[85] *U.S. For. Rel.*, 1922, I, 11.

[86] *American Law Review*, LVII:764ff (1923).

[87] League of Nations, *Official Journal*, 2nd year, no. 2:137 (March–April, 1921).

of the C mandates held by Great Britain, Australia, and New Zealand.[38] In reply a memorandum was sent to London in August 1921, detailing American grievances. First, the League's terms should be changed so that not only missionaries who were citizens of League member states, but also American missionaries, could be admitted. Second, since the treatment of mandates as integral portions of the mandatory's territory would permit discrimination, most-favored-nation treatment should be guaranteed. Third, grants of monopolistic concessions or the monopolization of natural resources by the mandatory itself should be prohibited. Fourth, any change in status of the C mandates should be subject to United States approval.[39]

Japan had made similar requests to Australia, objecting especially to the application of the "white Australia" policy to the mandates. Tokyo demanded not only equal opportunity for the future but preservation of all existing Japanese rights. The Commonwealth government was in a dilemma. The open door could not be granted to the United States and denied to Japan.[40] Here was an excellent opportunity for Secretary of State Hughes to take revenge on the Commonwealth for the Australian threat in Paris to stir up trouble on the West Coast over the race issue, and he did not miss the chance. He said to Balfour that he wished to discuss the mandate issue in a way most agreeable to the British mandatories. He knew, he continued, that Japan had also asked for the open door, and he would be happy to avoid the embarrassment to Australia and New Zealand that might well result from a joint discussion in which the Japanese and American positions would be similar.[41]

The threat was ineffective. The State Department received no answer to the August memorandum.[42] Worse still, statements in the Commonwealth parliament and new laws for

[38] *U.S. For. Rel.*, 1921, ii, 106.
[39] *Ibid.*, 108ff.
[40] *Japan Weekly Chronicle*, February 17, p. 213; February 24, p. 245; December 29, p. 938, 1921.
[41] *U.S. For. Rel.*, 1922, i, 11.   [42] *Ibid.*, 1921, ii, 115 *et al.*

the Australian mandates indicated that Australia had no intention of applying the open door. Australia's concept was that the mandatory could impose "whatever restrictions it pleased upon both men and goods."[43]

This had been Australia's attitude from the very beginning, and it had been approved by American statesmen. As early as May 1919 Prime Minister Hughes of Australia had written a letter to Colonel House in which he remarked that the difference between B and C mandates was one "of kind, not merely of degree," and that the C mandate "looks to its ultimate incorporation by the free will of its inhabitants."[44] In July 1919 during a session of the commission on mandates, the Japanese suggested the insertion of an open-door clause for the C mandates; the British representative objected on the basis that the guarantee of equal opportunity had been expressly excluded to appease the dominion prime ministers, and Colonel House agreed with the British view.[45] The Australians had thus good reason to consider their C mandates practically as good as ownership. Mr. Hughes represented Australian majority opinion in his peremptory statement that "there could be no open door in regard to the islands near Australia. There should be a barred and closed door— with Australia as the guardian of the door."[46] No answer was therefore given to the American memorandum of August. The next year, in July 1922, Washington followed up the memorandum with a note asking for an explanation.

London acknowledged receipt of the note and promised careful consideration in consultation with the dominions, but again there was no action.[47] So in October 1923 the United States government sent to London a draft proposal for an agreement on C mandates. The proposal was based on the "assumption that there is no difference in principle between

[43] *Ibid.*, 1923, II, 232ff.

[44] David Hunter Miller, *My Diary at the Peace Conference* (New York, 1924), IX, 290ff. This had been Wilson's idea also.

[45] *Ibid.*, XX:348.

[46] Australia, *Parliamentary Debates*, LXXXIX:12331, 12646, 12726; XCV:7352ff; Shepherd, *Australia's Interests*, 19.

[47] *U.S. For. Rel.*, 1923, II, 237.

the Government of the United States and the British Government as to the appropriate administration of mandate territories and my Government has had in mind the repeated disclaimers by your Lordship of any intention on the part of His Majesty's Government to deprive the United States of any of the rights and privileges to which it is entitled by the common victory over Germany or to discriminate against the United States nationals or companies."[48]

All along the American government tried to force Britain's hand by "assuming" that the stipulations which were clearly made for the A and B mandates would apply also to the C mandates. The British government had not committed itself on the C mandates, a fact that obviously disturbed Washington. The American *tour de force* this time was just as ineffective as on previous occasions. However, the long draft proposal showed Great Britain how important the question was to the United States, and at last produced a response.[49]

The problem of the open door in the C mandates was discussed during the imperial conference in the fall of 1923,[50] and in April 1925 an answer was finally sent to Washington by the British government on its own and the dominions' behalf. The answer was that the C mandates could not be treated like the other mandates for several reasons: First, the terms of the mandate made it an integral portion of the mandatory's territory. Second, the dominions had compromised on accepting mandates instead of insisting on annexation because the mandates were to be integral portions of the mandatory, and they would not go back on that agreement now. Third, a number of practical and physical reasons made it impossible for the dominions to grant America's wishes fully. However, the British government and the dominions were "willing that an assurance should be given, embodied, if desired, in the form of a binding engagement, that so long as the terms of the mandates remain

[48] *U.S. For. Rel.*, 1923, ii, 237ff.

[49] It was generally expected that Great Britain would accept the proposal. *New York Times*, November 18, 1923; *London Times*, November 12, 1923.

[50] *Imperial Conference, 1923*, Cmd. 1987 (1923), 15.

unaltered, United States nationals and goods will be treated in all respects on a footing equal to that enjoyed by the nationals and goods of any state member of the League of Nations, with the exception of those within the British Empire, subject only to the proviso that this shall not involve the violation of any existing treaty engagements towards third parties."[51] With this the United States had to be content.

Aside from this clarification of the status of C mandates, the years between 1921 and 1931 did not bring any new developments in the political relations between Australia and the United States. Australia was concentrating on internal social and economic developments; the United States did not feel the need for any changes in the southwest Pacific. Only another visit of an American naval squadron to Australia in 1925 aroused special interest in the otherwise quiet and uneventful relations between the two countries. The fleet visit was the occasion of even greater excitement than in 1908. For months ahead, the Australian press was preparing the people for the great event, and when the fleet finally arrived Australians went to extraordinary extremes to provide a reception for the American sailors.[52] The difference between the 1908 and 1925 visits was striking from a political standpoint. In 1908 the world situation was tense and the political significance of the fleet's cruise was obvious; in 1925 the world believed in collective security, and the fleet's visit was not accompanied by political suspicions.[53]

[51] *U.S. For. Rel.*, 1925, II, 216. Cf. Benjamin Gerig, *The Open Door and the Mandates System* (London, 1930).

[52] The details of the visit can be found in the contemporaneous newspapers, especially the *Sydney Morning Herald* between July 2 and August 7, 1925.

[53] See *Sydney Morning Herald*, March 28, 1925; *New York Times*, July 3, 1925.

CHAPTER X

American-Australian Economics

THE economic relations between the United States and Australia have had their ups and downs during the twentieth century, but have generally proceeded smoothly. One outstanding characteristic is the influence which Americans had upon the internal economic development of the Commonwealth. Advisers and technicians in various fields of economic activity visited Australia and contributed to the establishment of new industries, new methods of mining and agriculture, and improved communications.[1]

Australia also proved attractive to American financiers, especially in the early twenties when American capitalists looked for investment opportunities all over the world. Soon after World War I American capital could be found in the frozen-meat industry of northern Australia, in the mining of copper and coal, in the steel and electric industries, in land, and in experimentation for cotton-growing.[2] American penetration of the money market was somewhat more difficult, but eventually the British monopoly was broken. A loan for the state of Queensland in October 1921 was the first to be raised in the United States. The Queensland government was sharply criticized for this audacious undertaking and the high interest rate of 7 per cent was under special fire.[3] Nevertheless, New South Wales soon followed the Queensland precedent.[4] By 1924 the National City Bank and Blair and Company of New York had agents all over the continent offering capital for public loans or important commercial

[1] Australia, *Parliamentary Debates*, LXXIX:7819; "Some Problems of Australian Policy," *National Review*, XLV:722 (1905).

[2] W. P. Earsman, "The Pacific in World Politics," *Labour Monthly*, IV:238 (1923).

[3] *New York Times*, October 7, 11, 1921; *The Economist*, XCIII:575 (1921).

[4] Earsman, "The Pacific in World Politics," 238.

AUSTRALIA'S TRADE WITH THE UNITED STATES

FISCAL	Imports from U.S.A.		Exports to U.S.A.	
YEAR	VALUE IN £	PER CENT OF TOTAL	VALUE IN £	PER CENT OF TOTAL
1899–1903 ...	5,342,307	13.59	3,270,940	6.92
1904–8	5,124,191	11.55	2,483,637	3.87
1909–13	7,643,641	11.37	2,067,313	2.74
1914–15 to				
1918–19	16,720,033	21.82	9,807,368	11.44
1925–26	37,234,257	24.55	12,953,877	8.72
1928–29	35,308,345	24.58	5,831,794	4.03
1932–33	8,084,047	14.60	1,341,241	1.36
1935–36	13,901,705	17.05	5,615,372	4.51
1936–37	12,959,149	14.64	10,935,103	7.36
1938–39	14,647,305	15.09	3,614,038	2.95

enterprises.[5] In 1925 the Commonwealth government itself, with the approval of the British government, entered the American money market and successfully raised a loan of £15,000 at the lowest rate (5 per cent) ever granted to a foreign issue.[6] After this it became customary for Australians to raise funds abroad. In 1937, of a total external debt of £735,500,000 for the Commonwealth and states combined, £56,200,000 had been raised in New York and the remainder in London.[7] The total American investment in Australia, shortly before World War II, was estimated at one-half billion dollars. In 1945 the Australian government long-term debt in New York amounted to about two hundred million dollars with an average interest rate of about 5 per cent.[8]

The main feature of American-Australian trade has been its one-sidedness—America sends considerably larger quantities of goods to Australia than the Commonwealth is able to return. Since the beginning of this century Australian imports from America have been second only to those from the United Kingdom. The long-run trend has shown a constant improvement in this American position, while imports from Great Britain remained stationary or even declined occa-

[5] *London Times,* December 19, 20, 1924.
[6] *Sydney Morning Herald,* July 18, 20, 21, 22, 30, 1925.
[7] H. L. Harris, *Australia's National Interests and National Policy* (Melbourne, 1938), 116.
[8] Alexander, *Australia,* 45; *Sydney Morning Herald,* July 1, 1946.

sionally. On the other hand, the United States usually ranked only fourth to sixth among countries buying goods from Australia. In spite of frequent efforts to stimulate Australian exports to the United States, this unequal exchange remained the same.[9] Australia's staple exports are primary products such as wheat, wool, butter, milk, fruit, hides, and skins, which the United States also produces in abundance or can import cheaper from South American nations or excludes by tariff. Thus the major items of export to America—wool, animal skins, sausage casings—were bound to remain small in quantity. On the other hand, the United States has many manufactured or semi-manufactured articles and even primary products which Australia has to import. The major American products imported by Australia are tobacco, gasoline, oils, machinery, motor cars, and electrical appliances. While the industrialization of Australia and competition from Canada and Great Britain caused some change in the kinds of American exports to Australia, the steady flow of exports was never halted; instead, there has been a definite increase in the volume of exports.[10]

Australian attempts to rectify the one-sided trade with the United States have been as constant as they have been futile. Special efforts in this direction were made shortly after World War I when war-born industries cried for protection and returning soldiers demanded jobs. The Australian Tariff Act of 1921 and the preferential system for empire goods put great obstacles in the way of entry of American goods into Australia.[11] Yet a stream of American goods continued to flow into Australia and reached unprecedented heights between 1922 and 1930 as a result of the improved world economic situation.

Australia could afford large American imports and loans

[9] These conclusions were drawn from statistics in the *Official Year Book of the Commonwealth of Australia* covering the period under discussion.

[10] For details on American-Australian trade see, besides the usual official statistics, N. M. Windett, *Australia as Producer and Trader, 1920–1932* (Oxford, 1933), 263ff; Harris, *Australia's National Interests*, 82ff.

[11] Cf. *Literary Digest*, LXXIII:21 (June 10, 1922); LXXIX:17 (December 22, 1923).

because its export market was booming.[12] Primary producers obtained high prices for their goods and could sell them in unusually large quantities. Secondary industries—established with the help of protective tariffs—flourished. About one fourth of Australia's national income was derived from exports and foreign loans. Furthermore, prices for exports were high compared to prices for imports, a ratio favorable to Australia. The combination of these three factors—large exports, easy foreign loans, high export prices—combined to create prosperous conditions. The economic situation in the United States (and England) was equally favorable. Some doubts existed regarding the solidity of the boom and attempts were made to analyze its causes, but even though some warnings could be heard no heed was paid them. The general awakening and much hindsight wisdom arrived with the crash of 1929.

Australia's dependence on other countries for its economic welfare had quickly brought the boom and now equally quickly brought depression. Loans to Australia ceased, throwing the country on its own resources for carrying the debt burden and keeping the economy going. Export prices fell to extraordinarily low levels and the tariffs of other nations shut out Australian goods. The high tariff wall which the United States erected in 1930 and governmental obstructions to foreign trade by other countries were not as directly disadvantageous to Australia as the British undertaking to protect and subsidize the English farmer. Yet England could excuse itself by pointing to the dominion tariffs excluding British manufactured goods. Australia struggled valiantly and quite successfully to overcome its distress, but it could not do the job alone.

Everywhere it was quickly realized that the mutual exclusion of one another's goods would not lead to early re-

---

[12] For the following description of Australia's economic situation and the Ottawa agreement, these books have been consulted: Herbert Heaton, *The British Way to Recovery* (Minneapolis, 1934); Douglas B. Copland, *Australia in the World Crisis, 1929–1933* (New York, 1934); Douglas B. Copland and C. V. Janes, *Australian Trade Policy* (Sydney, 1937); Eric A. Walker, *The British Empire* (London, 1943).

covery and in the British empire this realization led to the Ottawa Conference in 1932. The main purpose of the conference was to stimulate trade among the members of the empire and to channel trade away from nonempire to empire countries.

Free trade within the empire was out of the question; the dominions would not agree to it. But the ideas of the representatives to the conference differed considerably. Great Britain desired a revival of trade not only for the benefit of the empire but also for the larger purpose of eliminating barriers to world trade. Most dominions did not take such a cosmopolitan view. South Africa was desirous of increasing trade among all members of the empire. Others, including Australia, were mainly interested in recapturing the British market in the dominions for their own products. There was considerable reluctance to comply with Great Britain's wishes, though eventually some concessions were made by the dominions.

The result of the conference was that to some degree and for a while all participants benefited. In Australia the controversy over the Ottawa agreement never died down. Basically, however, the agreement was accepted by most of the interested groups and the idea that British-Australian trade was of overriding importance to Australia's economy continued to have a strong hold on the people.

While admittedly the British market was of great importance to the Australian primary producer, two developments begun before Ottawa eventually made the Ottawa agreement anachronistic. One was the growing market for Australian products in Europe and the Far East, and the other the rapid growth of Australia's secondary industry. These new conditions required a reappraisal of Australia's position in the world economy, which, however, was not made until the late thirties. Against the background of world depression, the Ottawa agreement, and economic nationalism, Australia's trade diversion policy, inaugurated in 1936 just before the end of the Ottawa agreement, becomes understandable. This policy, which led to a small-scale trade war between the United States and Australia, was initiated after America refused to negotiate a reciprocal trade treaty.

Under the Trade Agreements Act of 1934, inaugurating the American reciprocity policy, the President was empowered to negotiate trade agreements with foreign powers and to reduce import duties up to 50 per cent without reference to Congress. The benefits granted to any country in an agreement accrued to all other countries having most-favored-nation relations with the United States. Australia was one of the first nations anxious to take advantage of the American act.[13] In June 1934 the Australian minister of commerce wrote to Washington describing the intolerable trade position —from Australia's standpoint—and urging the opening of negotiations for a trade pact.[14] No answer was received. Upon a further Australian note, the American government, in January 1935, sent a negative reply. Washington referred to its preoccupation with the negotiation of treaties with other powers and expressed doubt that the importation of Australian primary products could be increased.[15] A personal visit of Prime Minister Lyons to Washington in 1935 did not produce any better results. His conversations with American officials never went beyond broad generalities. The secretary of commerce told him that the United States could not very well buy primary products abroad while at the same time trying to reduce the production of such commodities within the country.[16]

The persistently negative American attitude irritated Australia. Washington concluded reciprocal treaties with a number of nations and even granted better treatment to nations which were poorer customers for American goods. America was accused of ignoring Australia's good buying record and of being unsympathetic to Australia.[17] Early in 1936 Sir Henry Gullett, minister in charge of treaties, informed the American consul-general that Australia would be forced to

[13] New York Times, December 22, 1937.
[14] Australia, Parliamentary Debates, CXLIX: 744ff.
[15] Ibid.   [16] Ibid.; New York Times, July 7, 9, 10, 1935.
[17] New York Times, April 3, 1936.

take arbitrary action if the United States could not negotiate with a view to adjusting the increasingly unfavorable trade balance.[18] Simultaneously the press announced that whatever Australia would do implied neither a punitive spirit nor the principle of equalization of trade but only a desire to divert trade to nations from which larger purchases might be expected.[19] On several occasions the Commonwealth government delayed its decision on restrictive measures in the hope of inducing the United States to negotiate, but without success.[20] Washington disliked the idea of Australian restrictions upon American trade but failed to do anything about it. The consul-general presented the American view to the Commonwealth government and pointed out that the Trade Agreements Act permitted the President to negotiate treaties only for the purpose of increasing existing markets.[21] This was, of course, no consolation to Australia. The Commonwealth government now realized that no treaty would be negotiated and proceeded with the inauguration of a restrictive policy.

On May 22, 1936, Sir Henry Gullett announced the government's trade diversion policy. The avowed object was the increase in exports of primary products, the expansion of secondary industries, and the creation of new rural and industrial employment. These aims were to be realized by the production of imported goods by home industries and the diversion of imports to "countries which are already great customers of ours." In justification of the policy Sir Henry remarked: "We have perforce to look to our exports to pay for our imports, and in the national interest we cannot allow our market for imports to be absorbed by countries which fail to extend a fair measure of reciprocity to the products of our export industries." The techniques to put the policy into practice were a licensing system and the imposition of prohibitive duties.[22]

The two countries most directly affected were the United

---

[18] Australia, *Parliamentary Debates*, CXLIX: 744.
[19] *New York Times*, April 17, 1936.   [20] *Ibid.*, April 7, 15, 1936.
[21] *Ibid.*, June 3, 1936; Australia, *Parliamentary Debates*, CXLIX: 744.
[22] *Ibid.*

States and Japan. Both struck back, the United States by withdrawing all benefits of lower tariff duties flowing from its reciprocal agreements with other nations. Australia was thus put on the same level as Germany, the only other country not receiving most-favored-nation treatment under the Trade Agreements Act.[23] The American consul-general half apologetically explained: "Unfortunately the application of the new Australian licensing system is discriminatory in relation to American trade, and in the circumstances we have been left with no choice but to withdraw all the trade benefits accruing under treaties."[24]

The trade diversion policy caused more general excitement in Australia (especially because of its repercussions in Japan) than in the United States. Australian opinion was divided on the merits of the new policy. Judgment was usually pronounced according to the particular interests of the judge.[25] The government seemed to be pleased with the result of its policy and tried to prove success by many figures and statistics.[26] The fact is that within a year after the inauguration of the new policy American wool buyers happened to acquire large quantities of Australian wool, which brought the Australian export figure close to the import figure. But after this wool-buying splurge, the import and export figures returned to their usual discrepancy. The success of the trade diversion could not be proved by trade statistics.[27]

In December 1937 Australia ended the trade diversion policy in relation to the United States and America restored Australia to the list of countries receiving most-favored-nation treatment.[28] There were reasons on both sides for the termination of the trade war. American exporters to Australia were eager to resume their trade,[29] and the American

[23] *New York Times,* June 30, 1936.

[24] Copland and Janes, *Australian Trade Policy,* 325.

[25] See the survey in Copland and Janes, *Australian Trade Policy,* 313, 328, 332, 341, 344.

[26] *Ibid.*

[27] *Ibid.,* pp. xx, 342, 345; *New York Times,* February 17, 18, 1937.

[28] *Ibid.,* December 9, 1937; January 28, 1938.

[29] Some exporters had established industries in Australia to make up for lost

government felt that the general improvement in world economic conditions, in addition to the American-British-French
currency agreement, eliminated the excuse for the trade diversion policy.[30] A section of the Australian cabinet never was
very happy over the trade war and wanted a change in the
policy. Australian manufacturers needed American machines
and tools, and the Australian people generally desired friendly relations with the United States in all their contacts.[31]
The negotiations for an Anglo-American trade agreement,
from which was expected not only improved trade relations
between those two countries but an improvement of the pro-
gressively deteriorating world political situation, prompted
both the United States and Australia to make any concessions short of what each considered essential national interests.[32]

Once friendly commercial relations between the two countries were re-established, the subject of a trade pact was
broached again. The possibility was discussed within the
cabinet of each nation, and between them, but negotiations
never reached the official stage. An agreement was found un-
feasible because the United States produced everything Australia had to export and this, by 1938, included a wide range
of products from secondary industries.[33]

The beginning of the war in 1939 changed the economic
situation in Australia and American-Australian relations
could no longer be considered normal. Australia's economy
was put on a war footing. In an endeavor to help the British
Commonwealth in the war effort, Australian industries were
developed to such an extent that people talked of "Australia's
industrial revolution." American machines and tools, especially the more expensive types, paid for in cash, contributed

sales. A. A. James, "Australia and the Anglo-U.S. Treaty," *Fortnightly*, cxlix:
183 (1938); *New York Times*, November 27, 1936.

[30] *Ibid.*, November 4, 5, 1936; December 22, 1937.

[31] *Ibid.*, November 27, 1936; February 7, November 11, December 6, 1937.

[32] *Ibid.*, June 12, November 11, 20, December 9, 1937; *Round Table*, xxvii:
849 (1937).

[33] *New York Times*, March 6, June 18, November 19, 29, December 21, 1938;
June 27, 1939; *Sydney Morning Herald*, January 24, 1938.

to this development.[34] Australia expected much material help from the United States. The Lend-Lease Act was greeted with enthusiasm in the Commonwealth when it became law in 1941. The acting prime minister stated that the act "would become as vital for us and for our children as Magna Charta and the Bill of Rights."[35] The act was unilateral and permitted the President of the United States for the better defense of the country to provide American war materials and supplies on lend-lease terms to countries whose security was essential to the safety of the United States. Many months before any bilateral agreement was signed, the United States shipped lend-lease goods to Great Britain and as early as September 1941 Britain, with American approval, diverted some of these goods to Australia.[36] On November 11, 1941, President Roosevelt declared Australia vital for the defense of the United States, which permitted the sending of lend-lease goods to Australia direct.[37]

On February 23, 1942, Great Britain and the United States concluded a mutual aid agreement on a lend-lease basis in which Australia participated indirectly as a member of the British Commonwealth. But even before the signing of this master agreement, the Australian minister in Washington broached the question of lend-lease supplies and his preliminary conversations were continued when Evatt arrived in Washington in March 1942. Simultaneously an American mission went to Australia to discuss the same problems. The result of these contacts was the establishment of an Allied Supply Council in Australia—an Australian idea—composed of members of the Commonwealth government, the American army, and the lend-lease organization. The purpose of the council was to develop Australia into a major supply and

[34] Wilson C. Flake, "Australia," *Foreign Commerce Weekly,* XVII : 37 (December 16, 1944). Cf. Harry MacNamara, "Australia and the United Nations," *Amerasia,* VII : 337 (1943); *Amerasia,* IX : 11 (1945).

[35] Australia, *Parliamentary Debates,* CLXVI : 118f.

[36] Howard Daniel and Minnie Belle, "Australia and Lend-Lease," *Far Eastern Survey,* XII : 233 (1943).

[37] President's *Twentieth Report to Congress on Lend-Lease Operations* (Washington, August 30, 1945).

operation base for the Pacific war theater. It coordinated procurement for the United Nations forces, increased Australian production, and determined broad economic policies for the southwest Pacific area.[38]

On September 3, 1942, Australia and the United States signed a reciprocal lend-lease agreement in which the principles of the master agreement between the United Kingdom and the United States were recognized and in which Australia promised to provide three categories of supplies: first, military equipment, ammunition, and military and naval stores; second, other supplies, materials, facilities, and service; and third, supplies, materials, and services needed in the construction of military projects and similar capital works required for the common war effort either within or without Australian territory.[39] This agreement completed the formal legal framework within which reciprocal lend-lease between the United States and Australia could function. But just as American lend-lease supplies had been flown into Australia before any formal agreement had been signed, so Australian reciprocal lend-lease goods went to United States forces long before September 1942.

Australian aid began when a call came from Bataan for ten thousand tons of processed food. The food was shipped and some of it reached its destination.[40] Thus mutual lend-lease aid between the two nations existed very soon after Pearl Harbor. America mostly supplied weapons and machinery of all kinds and petroleum products. Australia reciprocated with food supplies above all else, but it also provided uniforms, shoes, blankets, services—especially in the field of transportation and communication—buildings of all kinds, small war vessels, and ammunition. Most of these supplies were used in Australia, but many were shipped to the American forces in the southwest Pacific. The amount of aid Aus-

[38] U.S. Department of State, *Bulletin*, viii : 66 (1943) ; Edward R. Stettinius, *Lend-Lease* (New York, 1944), chap. xv.

[39] For the text of this agreement see Department of External Affairs, *Current Notes on International Affairs* (Canberra), xiii : 63 (1942).

[40] Edward R. Stettinius, Jr., *Report to the 78th Congress on Lend-Lease Operations* (January 25, 1943), 51.

tralia gave was remarkable considering the size of the population. It was achieved only by the willingness of the Australian people to sacrifice and to subject themselves voluntarily to the strictest government controls in every aspect of their social life.[41]

The amount of American lend-lease supplies decreased in the later period of the war. Three reasons accounted for this. Largely with initial American machine supplies, Australian domestic production increased; Australia had on hand large stockpiles which it could use up; and America supplied Australia with military goods on a basis of current replacements rather than with the idea of creating reserves. On June 8, 1946, an American-Australian agreement announced the termination of lend-lease and reciprocal aid. The United States had given Australia £A388,000,000 in goods and services, and Australia reciprocated with £A261,000,000.[42] The United States agreed to settle for £A8,400,000, which was recognized by Australia as very generous. But, as Prime Minister Curtin had remarked, the ratio of exchange was much less important than the fact that both countries contributed to the maximum of their capacity.

Commercial relations between the two nations were on a most friendly basis during the war years. In 1943 the Commonwealth government voluntarily granted the United States most-favored-nation treatment, which until that time had only been granted by America to the Commonwealth.[43] This was more a gesture than anything else, since civilian exchange of goods was limited, not only because of war conditions but also because the heavy cash purchases of machines and tools from the United States before 1941 had depleted Australian dollar funds.[44]

While the abnormally large exchange of goods and serv-

---

[41] *Ibid.* Cf. Flake, "Australia," *Foreign Commerce Weekly*, xvii: 5f (December 9, 1944); *Commonweal*, xxxix: 464 (1944).

[42] President's *Twentieth Report*. Detailed statistics regarding the type, quantity, and value of goods and services exchanged can be found in the frequent reports about lend-lease to Congress.

[43] *Current Notes*, xiv: 93 (1943); *New York Times*, June 11, 1946.

[44] Flake, "Australia," *Foreign Commerce Weekly*, xvii: 37 (December 16, 1944).

ices between the two countries ceased with the end of the war and of lend-lease, both favorable and unfavorable results of the close economic contacts will remain. Australian agricultural production and secondary industries were increased tremendously during the war years. Australia will need export markets, which it cannot find in sufficient size within the British empire, and more than ever, is looking toward the Far Eastern and southeastern Asiatic nations as potential customers. The United States is looking in the same direction, and there is a possible source of friction in competition between the two nations. However, Australians realize that these Asiatic areas will have to be developed before they can become a really attractive market, and the United States will admittedly have to play a major role in that development. Australians hope that an enlightened American policy will permit Australian participation in the potentially large consumer market of the Far East.[45]

As far as the direct trade relations between the two nations are concerned, the problem of one-sidedness still exists, and may even be aggravated by the results of the war. Through lend-lease aid, much of Australian industry is geared to American machinery, standards, and practices. Most likely Australia will continue to import American machinery at the expense of British imports, a trend which existed before the war. This means an increase of American imports into Australia that cannot be balanced by the reduction of imports of articles which Australia may now be able to produce itself. A very rigorous exclusion of American goods may enable Australia to adjust its unfavorable balance. But this reduction would be at the expense of the total volume of trade between the two countries, which neither desires. A very careful search for products that each nation could buy from the other might permit the conclusion of a trade agreement which

[45] Australian Institute of International Affairs, *Australia and the Pacific* (Princeton, 1944), 139ff; James P. Belshaw, "Markets for Australian Exports," *Far Eastern Survey*, xiv:58 (1945); Ethel B. Dietrich, *Far Eastern Trade of the United States* (New York, 1940), 90; Clunies Ross, ed., *Australia and the Far East*, 172, 185; W. G. K. Duncan, ed., *Australia's Foreign Policy* (Sydney, 1938), chap. ii; Foreign Minister Evatt in the *Sydney Morning Herald*, February 1, 1943.

would promote a fairly even exchange of goods, although the total volume on such a basis will always remain small. The Australian minister for external affairs, Evatt, restated the problem late in 1945 when he was in New York to open the first consular offices established by the Commonwealth abroad. If America wants to trade, he said, it will have to take Australian goods. Australia must earn dollars in order to be able to buy; "unless we can earn more here, we may have to do with less of your excellent products or make more of them for ourselves. In short, traffic between our two countries in their commodities must be two-way traffic."

The problem of obtaining dollars will remain a major difficulty in American-Australian trade relations. Canberra is trying to reduce the Australian dollar debt in order to save the precious exchange on interest payments, which amount to about three million Australian pounds annually. Before World War II Australia was able to acquire dollars from London. It is doubtful that the American loan to Great Britain will again open up this source of supply.

The projected Trade and Employment Conference at Paris, in which the United States, Great Britain, and Australia will take part, may solve some of the problems of international trade. But the Australian government has already announced that it will do everything to maintain the present system of empire preference. This policy may not agree with American ideas on an unhampered flow of goods between nations.[46] Before a free and equal exchange of goods between the two nations can be realized, the field of finance and industrial assistance may become more important in American-Australian relations. Australians, eager to expand war-developed industries, are looking to the United States for capital, machinery, and experts. The visit of Australian statesmen to the United States in the summer of 1946 was concerned mainly with the discussion of economic matters of greatest concern to Australia.[47]

[46] *Australia,* v (November 1945); *Sydney Morning Herald,* June 29, July 1, 1946; *New York Times,* September 14, 1946.
[47] *New York Times,* March 15, April 15, 1946. Cf. Howard Daniel and Minnie Belle, *Australia, The New Customer* (New York, 1946).

CHAPTER XI

War in the Pacific

THE decade from 1931 to 1941 was characterized in the Pacific as elsewhere by the breakdown of the system of collective security. The process was gradual, and as it advanced Australians became disturbed about their fate in the Pacific. Australia was one of the smaller nations which had great faith in the various treaties designed to preserve peace in the world. The "Manchuria incident" in 1931 was the first warning of the deterioration of the international situation. Since this event coincided with a rapid improvement of Australian-Japanese trade, desperately needed by primary producers in the Commonwealth, it seemed unwise to antagonize a good actual, and an even better potential, customer. From a broader viewpoint Australians could see no sense in provoking Japan into a war with the British Commonwealth for the sake of faraway China. In fact, many Australians preferred that Japan should direct imperialistic ambitions toward China rather than toward the southwest Pacific.[1]

Throughout the crisis the Commonwealth government kept in close touch with London and favored every British effort at conciliation, but otherwise felt that the less said about the affair the better. There was not one ministerial statement about taking any line of action either prescribed or possible under the collective security system. There was no mention of Australia's special interests in the Far Eastern situation, and the minister for external affairs did his best to discourage any discussion about the potentialities of the situation.[2]

Public opinion on the issue was confused. While the Labour press was critical of Japan, many newspapers either

---

[1] Alexander, *Australia*, 23ff; Shepherd, *Australia's Interests*, 36ff; W. Macmahon Ball, ed., *Press, Radio, and World Affairs* (Melbourne, 1938), chap. II, gives an excellent survey of press opinion on Japan's action.

[2] *Round Table*, XXIII:684 (1933).

took no stand at all or were inconsistent in their opinion. No serious appraisal of Japan's basic Far Eastern policy was made; the perennial theme of the "Asiatic menace" was brought forth, but this was as unconstructive and ineffective as the shouts of the man crying wolf. American policy was scrutinized mainly from the angle of Australian security: Will the United States implement its protests with force? The answer seemed to be in the negative, and Australians therefore preferred not to run any risks and willingly agreed with their government's do-nothing policy.

Subsequent indications of Japan's intentions in the Far East and "Greater East Asia" changed the vague uneasiness of the Australian people into mild alarm. The clever play of various Australian interests upon the traditional fears and suspicions of the people succeeded in interfering with the official policy of friendship, and prepared the field for the trade diversion policy in 1936 that administered a blow to economic and consequently political relations between Japan and Australia from which these relations never quite recovered.[3] The government faced many difficulties in the following years, but it remained optimistic and was supported by many influential groups in Australia.[4]

The renewed attack of Japan upon China in 1937 provoked a more united opposition in Australia to Japan's action than the 1931 incident. The atmosphere had changed. The Manchuria incident had been a single catastrophe in an otherwise peaceful era of collective security. By 1937 a chain of events had taken place which destroyed reliance on the peace treaties for the most sanguine optimists. Australian public opinion clearly condemned Japanese aggression.

However, as the Sino-Japanese war progressed and became an everyday affair, the public lost interest.[5] A typical press comment in 1939 upon the situation ran as follows: "A hope-

[3] Cf. Shepherd, *Australia's Interests*, chap. III.

[4] E.g., R. G. Casey, "Australia in World Affairs," *Australian National Review*, II:2 (July 1937); Clunies Ross, ed., *Australia*, 185.

[5] Ball, ed., *Press, Radio, and World Affairs*, 50ff; Shepherd, *Australia's Interests*, 72ff.

ful sign for the future is that Japan is prepared to purchase two-thirds of her wool requirements from Australia . . . On the other hand, the military policy of Japan is somewhat disturbing, particularly in view of the uncertainty of British naval power in the Pacific."[6] Only a few individuals especially interested in the foreign affairs of their country continued serious debate of the issue. Their opinions were very diverse and they failed to agree upon a desirable foreign policy for Australia.[7]

The Commonwealth government experienced similar difficulties, but was forced to adopt some policy. Since a valiant Australian attempt in 1936 to restore collective security in the Pacific had been frustrated by Japan's aggression, the government decided to follow the precedent from 1931: it did nothing politically, in fact leaned over backwards to avoid provoking Japan, and tried to rebuild Australian-Japanese trade to its former volume. In view of the fact that the major western powers pursued a policy toward Japan which could not encourage Australia to run the slightest risk, the government's policy was reasonable.

While conducting an appeasement policy toward Japan, the Commonwealth government prepared for the day when this policy would prove futile. From 1937 on Australia engaged in a defense program which grew into extraordinary proportions as the political situation in Europe became worse. The program envisaged an augmentation of all fighting forces, a development of fortifications, harbor facilities, and overland communications, a provision for the accumulation of primary products as emergency reserves, and finally the reshaping of Australian economy on a war footing.[8] When the European war broke out in 1939, Australia was well advanced in war preparation.

United States policy in 1931 and after gave little encouragement for a strong Australian stand, nor indeed did it provide any possibility for cooperation between the two nations

---

[6] *Australian National Review*, vi:2 (July 1939).

[7] Duncan, ed., *Australia's Foreign Policy*, chap. iii.

[8] Shepherd, *Australia's Interests*, 97ff.

against what both expected to be a common enemy. American policy during the Manchuria incident consisted mainly in diplomatic protests to Japan and appeals to fulfill international obligations, with no intention of implementing political action by force.[9] American policy between 1933 and 1937 might be described as an attempt to restrain Japan short of running risks. Continuation of the nonrecognition doctrine, establishment of diplomatic relations with Russia, fleet maneuvers west of Hawaii, and some naval rearmament, did not prevent Japan from blasting one Washington agreement after another and thus destroying collective security in the Pacific.

The renewed Japanese aggression in 1937 found the United States in an isolationist mood and unwilling to protect its traditional policy of the open door and China's integrity with more than protests. Until July 1939 American diplomacy was "extraordinarily patient and conciliatory."[10] In the United States, as in Australia, the reluctance to adopt strong measures against Japan was coupled with a weak and somewhat belated rearmament program. In addition to some naval rearmament the government sponsored Pacific air routes and supported recommendations for the development of air and naval bases in the Pacific. Indirectly, the American government hampered Japanese success by financial and material aid to China.[11]

Australia looked in vain for leadership in a policy to curb Japanese aggression. Though there was growing parallelism in diplomacy in the Far East between America and Great Britain after 1939, there were no overtures for effective common action from any of the big powers.[12] The increasing vigor of American protests to Japan and President Roosevelt's demand for larger armament expenditures on January

[9] For details see the relevant chapters in Harold S. Quigley and George H. Blakeslee, *The Far East* (Boston, 1938); T. A. Bisson, *America's Far Eastern Policy* (New York, 1945); Griswold, *Far Eastern Policy.*

[10] Harold S. Quigley, *Far Eastern War, 1937-1941* (Boston, 1942), 211.

[11] *Ibid.,* 202ff.

[12] Australia participated in the activities of the League of Nations and the Brussels Conference.

29, 1938, caused great satisfaction in Australia.[13] However, Australians were careful not to draw rash conclusions from the firmer American attitude—America was "the enigma of the Pacific."[14] Guesses as to the possible American reaction to a British-Japanese war were made in abundance, but the absence of convincing answers only emphasized the existing uncertainty and caused a good deal of anxiety. Even the faith that the Anglo-Saxon "cousins" would not let Australia perish lost some of its hold over the people. Former Prime Minister Hughes, in a visit to the United States in 1936, had found that there the Anglo-Saxon race was "slipping."[15] And a member of the Commonwealth parliament branded all talk of common origin as pure nonsense. The United States, he said, "has a most uncommon origin. Its people have come from every one of these quibbling, squabbling Central European States"; there was no common outlook in the United States.[16] Nevertheless most Australians took some comfort in the common origin theory and the pronounced tendency of the United States to side with the democracies.[17]

The more political conditions decayed, the more Australia became aware of its isolation in the Pacific. The government felt a great need to substitute some system of cooperation for the vanished collective security. Prime Minister Menzies gave expression to this desire when he said, "I look forward to the day when we will have a concert of Pacific powers, pacific in both senses of the word. This means increased diplomatic contacts between ourselves and the United States, China, and Japan, to say nothing of the Netherlands East Indies and the other countries which fringe the Pacific."[18] In preparation for this important step, an Australian liaison

[13] *Sydney Morning Herald*, January 31, 1938.

[14] Duncan, ed., *Australia's Foreign Policy*, 94.

[15] For Hughes's recent attitudes see Dorsey W. Jones, "The Foreign Policy of William Morris Hughes of Australia," *Far Eastern Quarterly*, II:153ff (1942).

[16] Australia, *Parliamentary Debates*, May 9, 1939, p. 224; cf. *New York Times*, January 25, 1942 (sec. I).

[17] Australia, *Parliamentary Debates*, May 9, 1939, pp. 197, 235; May 17, 1939, p. 372; August 6, 1940, p. 194.

[18] *Ibid.*, May 31, 1939, p. 953; cf. *ibid.*, May 9, 1939, pp. 199, 214; May 17, 1939, pp. 373, 375, 383.

officer had been attached to the British embassy in Washington since 1937, and the Australian commissioner in New York had been replaced by a commissioner-general. Early in January 1940 the appointment of R. G. Casey as the first Australian minister to the United States and the reciprocal appointment of Clarence E. Gauss from the United States was officially announced.[19]

A minister in Washington now enabled the Commonwealth to present its views on the Pacific directly and forcibly. He arrived in the capital in time to participate in discussions between the American and British governments which led to a growing solidarity between the two nations. The political and military events in Europe, as well as the clear indications of Japan's intention to move southward and into southeastern Asia, provided the background for this development. This threat to southeastern Asia was a threat to life lines of the British empire and to vital raw materials needed for the survival of Great Britain, which the United States considered vital for its own safety. Anything endangering the existence of Great Britain was therefore considered as indirectly endangering the United States. Consequently, Japan's southward move immediately provoked a stiffer attitude on the part of the United States and the planning of measures to prevent the realization of Japan's intentions.[20]

A preliminary arrangement between the United States and Great Britain in this direction had been made in the spring of 1939, when the two powers agreed upon a condominium over Canton and Enderbury islands to be used as air fueling stations. This agreement showed, in the words of Churchill, that the "principle of association of interests for common purposes between Great Britain and the United States had developed even before the war."[21] During 1940 this association received its strongest impetus.

[19] *Sydney Morning Herald,* January 9, 10, 1940; Australia, *Parliamentary Debates,* August 6, 1940, pp. 188, 208, 211.

[20] This statement is based on *U.S. For. Rel., Japan 1931–1941,* II.

[21] Hansard, *Parliamentary Debates,* CCCLXIV:1170 (1940); *New York Times,* August 21, 1940.

At first there were no official announcements of any special preparations going on in the Pacific and the public had to be content with speculations. The purpose of the Pacific fleet's presence in Hawaii after the spring maneuvers, for instance, was a subject of much discussion. The President's explanations were vague and failed to clear up the puzzling situation.[22] In Australia, America remained an enigma, but the presence of the fleet in Hawaii was considered a safeguard against danger in the Pacific. This view was confirmed by Australians who had learned in Washington that neither Australia's nor Singapore's fate was a matter of indifference to the United States.[23] This was an excellent prop to Australian morale, which rested essentially on two factors: the success of their own war effort and the safety of Singapore. There were rumors about the possible use of Singapore by the American fleet. In Japan it was said (after the United States delivered fifty destroyers to Great Britain) that the Atlantic defense would be left to Great Britain and the Pacific defense to the United States, and that for this purpose America and Australia were planning a defense agreement. One thing was certain in this uncertainty: the Pacific was in a "stage of definite development."[24]

Soon the riddle was partly solved by official announcements in various quarters. Since the fall of 1940 conversations had been going on between Great Britain, the United States, and Australia aiming at the coordination of defense in the Pacific. The use of Singapore and Australian bases, as well as broader questions of strategy and Far Eastern policy, were discussed. Agreement was reached to such an extent that detailed emergency decisions could be made on short notice. The Commonwealth government was optimistic and announced that the "firm and sympathetic attitude adopted by the United States of America has been of immeasurable

22 *Ibid.*, June 23, 1940.
23 *Ibid.*, August 22, 1940.
24 *London Times*, September 5, 6, 1940.

assistance to the Commonwealth in the formulation and application of its Far Eastern policy."[25]

This agreement on general principles was quickly implemented with more detailed arrangements. Increasingly, American ships carried empire goods across the Pacific through the Panama Canal to Atlantic Coast ports, where British ships took them to Great Britain (American vessels being prevented from sailing to Great Britain by neutrality legislation), thus relieving British shipping of duty in the Pacific. In June 1941 this system was put on an organized basis. American vessels handled all British shipping services between the United States and Canada and Australia and New Zealand. In the late summer of 1941 landing strips at Rabaul, Port Moresby, and Port Darwin were improved, and gasoline and bombs were shipped to these points. The help of the Australian government in the development of this air route from the United States to the Philippines, used mostly by heavy bombers, was of great value in the attempt later on to stem the wave of Japanese advance.[26]

During their meeting on the Atlantic in August 1941, Roosevelt and Churchill discussed the situation in the Pacific at some length, and Churchill seemed much encouraged by these talks. He explained to the President that Great Britain was obliged to use its forces in the west and hardly expected a Japanese attack when it had failed to materialize after Dunkirk, though there was no certainty regarding Japanese plans. "The probability, since the Atlantic Conference, at which I discussed these matters with Mr. Roosevelt," reported Churchill to Parliament in January 1942, "that the United States, even if not herself attacked, would come into a war in the Far East, and thus make final victory sure, seemed

[25] Australia, *Parliamentary Debates*, CLXV:251ff; also *ibid.*, CLXV:476; *New York Times*, November 8, 1940. In March and August 1941 American naval detachments visited Australia and received the usual enthusiastic reception. This time some political significance was attached to the visit, whereas a previous visit in 1938 was a courtesy call on the occasion of Australia's 150th anniversary.

[26] *New York Times*, June 4, 1941; General George C. Marshall, *Biennial Report on the Army*, July 1, 1941, to June 30, 1943, the Third Phase.

to allay some of these anxieties. That expectation has not been falsified by the events. It fortified our British decision to use our limited resources on the actual fighting fronts. As time went on, one had greater assurance that if Japan ran amok in the Pacific, we should not fight alone."[27]

The initial contact between American and British defense forces in the Far East was established by the arrival of Air Chief Marshall Sir Robert Brooke-Popham from Singapore in Manila in April 1941. He discussed defense plans with the highest American officers there, and proceeded to Australia where he completed his mission of clarifying America's role and coordinating Far Eastern defense against the Axis powers.

At the end of Sir Robert's trip Prime Minister Curtin of Australia announced that the "full democratic forces" were now cooperating in the Pacific. Australia, he continued, had taken several important steps for cooperation with other powers in the Pacific, "reflecting an extraordinary advance on what might have been considered possible a year ago."[28] The next day he followed up this announcement by a statement to the effect that negotiations had been completed for a united front in the Pacific between Great Britain, the United States, China, the Netherlands Indies, Australia, and New Zealand, promising cooperation to a "substantial" degree.[29] Hallett Abend, the *New York Times* correspondent, supplemented this official statement by a report from Australia about the existing cooperation between America and Australia, New Zealand, the Netherlands, and Singapore, which, he said, "would astound the general, uninformed American public."[30] This solidarity among the Pacific powers was heartening to Australians. Nevertheless, their dissatisfaction with the conduct of the war soon after Pearl Harbor showed that the broad agreements were not sufficient and that many matters, unexpectedly perhaps, remained to be settled.

[27] Hansard, *Parliamentary Debates*, cccLxxvii : 607 (1942).
[28] *New York Times*, October 20, 1941.   [29] *Ibid.*, October 21, 1941.
[30] *Ibid.*, October 29, 1941; cf. Stettinius, *Lend-Lease*, 179.

On December 27, 1941, Prime Minister Curtin wrote an article for the *Melbourne Herald* which set the keynote for Australia's policy in the Pacific war and caused a sensation in empire circles. The Pacific war was not a side issue, Curtin wrote. Admittedly, "Australia looks to America free from pangs about our traditional links of friendship with Britain. . . . We shall exert our energy towards shaping a plan with the United States as its keystone, giving our country confidence and ability to hold out until the tide of battle swings against the enemy." In the Pacific war "the United States and Australia should have the fullest say in the direction of the fighting plan."[31] Simultaneously President Roosevelt announced that America would assist Australia and make it an operational base for American forces.[32] From then on the Commonwealth devoted its energy to a realization of the aims broadly outlined in Curtin's article.

By January 5, 1942, the United States and Great Britain had unified and coordinated their military and naval supplies, their shipping facilities, and the command of naval forces in the Atlantic. They had created a joint advisory board of military and naval experts for the study of worldwide strategy and coordinated all Washington and London offices dealing with the war effort. The southwest Pacific command was unified under Field Marshall Sir Archibald Wavell, and encompassed the islands and the north shore of Australia.[33]

The rapid advance of the Japanese apparently was unexpected and the agreements reached in pre-Pearl Harbor days did not provide sufficiently for the emergency. The saving of Australia as a base for operations became imperative and urgent. General George C. Marshall afterward described the situation thus: "In view of the enemy's capabilities throughout the Pacific and our untenable position in the

[31] Curtin disclosed in this article that he had asked London for a Russo-British pact of assistance in case of a Japanese attack, but that the request was refused as "premature."

[32] *New York Times,* December 29, 1941.

[33] *Ibid.,* January 5, 6, 1942.

Philippines, the major efforts of the United States were directed toward a rapid concentration of defense forces along our route to Australia, the creation of an effective striking force on that continent and the dispatch of material aid to the forces of our allies in the East Indies." Australia became of outstanding importance for American strategy and security.[34]

After Pearl Harbor American men and materiel poured into Australia.[35] Australians were naturally pleased with this concrete proof of American help and even more so with the American-British solidarity evidenced in the unification and coordination of their war effort, but this was not enough. The Australian government wanted to play an active part, and demanded loudly and persistently a place on any control council which might be established to deal with Pacific affairs. London tried to appease Canberra with an assurance that senior Australian officers would have an opportunity to participate in discussions of Wavell's command. Still the Australian government was not satisfied. In a note to London the prime minister made two specific requests. First, he demanded Australian representation in an imperial war cabinet in London; second, he demanded "that a Pacific War Council should be established on which countries particularly concerned with the Pacific might collaborate in dealing with the war problems in that theatre," and that this council should have its seat in Washington. New Zealand supported the request but had only a "preference" for Washington.[36]

The first demand was granted, though with certain restrictions.[37] The second demand created some political difficulty. Great Britain was unwilling to grant it. Churchill consulted Roosevelt, who had been directly informed by the Australian

[34] Stettinius, *Lend-Lease*, 171; *New York Times*, January 25, 1942.

[35] See pp. 154f.

[36] *Sydney Morning Herald*, January 12, 1942; *New York Times*, January 13, 25 (sec. i), 26, 27; Hansard, *Parliamentary Debates*, cccLxxvii:611ff (1942).

[37] Owing to certain objections from Canada and South Africa, the Commonwealth representative had no voice in the London cabinet; see *New York Times*, January 28, 30, 31, 1942; *Manchester Guardian Weekly*, February 6, 1942, p. 83.

minister, on this point in conjunction with other problems affecting the general organization of the war effort.[38] Out of these discussions in January 1942 emerged the basic organization of the Allies for the conduct of the war.

The Combined Chiefs of Staff Committee, established in Washington, consisted of the very highest United States military officers and a high representative of each of the British fighting services. The task of the committee was to insure complete coordination of the war effort and also to provide the full Anglo-American cooperation with the United Nations associated in the prosecution of the war. A liaison was thus provided for Australia to "participate with the Combined Chiefs of Staff in the consideration of matters concerning their national interest."[39]

A Pacific council was established in London, consisting of representatives of the British Commonwealth and the Netherlands. Its task was to coordinate views on the Pacific war and to transmit the result to the Combined Chiefs of Staff Committee in Washington. The London council would be advisory in character; Washington would make the decisions. Purely military or naval matters would go to Washington exclusively, where the Combined Chiefs of Staff Committee would consult with Australian, New Zealand, and Netherlands officers, and then decide. In case of conflict between the London council and the Washington committee, Roosevelt and Churchill would be the arbiters.[40]

This was clumsy machinery, bound to produce delay and friction, and obviously a compromise to satisfy Australia and other Pacific nations that had supported Australia's demand for a stronger voice in Pacific affairs. The only plausible explanation appears to be London's extreme reluctance to transfer control of Pacific strategy to American hands.[41] Aus-

[38] *Ibid.*, January 23, 1942, p. 52; *New York Times*, January 27, 28, 1942.

[39] *Ibid.*, February 7, 1942; *Current Notes*, xiv : 24 (1943); Hansard, *Parliamentary Debates*, ccclxxvii : 611ff (1942).

[40] *Ibid.; New York Times*, February 7, 10, 13, 1942. A Combined Raw Materials Board, a Shipping Adjustment Board, and a Munitions Assignment Board were also created at this time. *Current Notes*, xiv : 25 (1943).

[41] Lord Strabolgi, *Singapore and After* (London, 1942), 97.

tralia did not accept the compromise.[42] In February 1942 Australia was in no mood to pay respect to high politics. Australia was fighting for its life; the Pacific war was primarily an American-Australian affair and was to be run by those two powers from Washington. Prime Minister Curtin continued to work for a Pacific war council in Washington. The fall of Singapore, pivot of Australia's defense,[43] gave added impetus to his campaign.

Toward the end of February 1942, when the danger of invasion had moved uncomfortably close, the Australian and New Zealand governments met in conference. They planned a new strategic area, to include Australia and New Zealand, and decided to entrust supreme operational command in the new area to a United States officer. On February 22 Prime Minister Curtin requested President Roosevelt to give General MacArthur the supreme direction of the war in the Australian zone.[44]

Early in March, H. V. Evatt, the Australian minister for external affairs, went to Washington to discuss the Australian–New Zealand plan and to plead for all possible assistance. He was successful. With the modification that the new strategic area was to be subdivided into two, the President gave him a promise that the area would come under American command and a statement in which the United States accepted "responsibility" for Australia and New Zealand.[45]

Evatt's second major purpose for being in Washington was the creation of a Pacific war council in Washington. In view of the threat to Australia's security as a consequence of the defeat of the British Navy and the fall of Singapore, it was quite natural that Australia should turn to the United States for assistance. Yet the urgent Australian call for help from America—beginning with Curtin's article and growing as Japan approached Australian shores—caused some astonishment and resentment in Great Britain and was not wholly

[42] *New York Times*, February 10, 13, 1942.
[43] See *Australia*, I (January 1942); Australia, *Parliamentary Debates*, May 9, 17, 1939; *Sydney Morning Herald*, February 12, 1942.
[44] *Current Notes*, XIII:55 (1942).   [45] *Ibid.*

acceptable even to some Australians. The Commonwealth government was obliged to spend precious time and energy to assure its own people and some others at regular intervals that leanings toward the United States did not imply any desire for separation from the British empire, let alone to become the forty-ninth state. At the most some Australian statements at that time could be interpreted as expressions of anger at the lack of foresight and preparation on the part of Great Britain.[46]

Evatt's work for establishment of the council was prepared for by a radio broadcast of the prime minister in which he expressed regret that "even now, after ninety-five days of Japan's staggering advance south, we have not obtained first-hand contact with America."[47] Evatt in Washington was outspoken about his country's dissatisfaction with the political coordination of the war effort as it affected the Pacific theater. He pleaded for a Pacific war council in Washington in which Australia and the other Pacific powers should be accepted as allies on an equal footing. Australia's views were not necessarily to prevail, but they should be heard. He even went farther and, again with New Zealand's support, demanded the formation of a supreme war council of the United Nations in Washington.

Toward the end of March Evatt's endeavors proved successful. A Pacific war council was created, consisting of the United States, Great Britain, Australia, New Zealand, Canada, China, and the Netherlands, with headquarters in Washington. The Washington council was to take precedence over the London council, which was reduced to the role of liaison between the views of the Washington council and the British government. London accepted the new arrangement with good grace, rationalizing that the appointment of MacArthur as United Nations commander in the southwest Pacific and

---

[46] E.g., *New Statesman and Nation*, xxiii:1 (1942); *New York Times*, January 17, 1942; *Manchester Guardian Weekly*, February 6, p. 89, March 13, p. 166, March 27, p. 201, 1942; cf. William Yandell Elliott and H. Duncan Hall, eds., *The British Commonwealth at War* (New York, 1943), 402ff.

[47] *New York Times*, March 14, 1942.

the fall of Singapore and Malaya made the Pacific war mostly an American responsibility and that the creation of the Pacific war council in Washington simply reflected the shifting of the center of forces arrayed against Japan.[48] President Roosevelt stressed the fact that the Pacific war council had merely advisory functions and was a consultative body.[49] He was apparently anxious for Australia to know the exact limitations of the council's power. Nevertheless in practice the council developed into something more than a mere debating society, at least at first, in the days when the military situation looked worst. A number of questions of a political character and to some extent also of a military character were definitely decided at council meetings.[50]

On March 17, 1942, General MacArthur arrived in Australia and on the same day, in accordance with Australia's request, he was appointed supreme commander of the United Nations' forces in the southwestern Pacific. His arrival and appointment were greeted with great jubilation by Australians and the United Nations.[51] It was now evident that Australia had become the major base of operations for the Allied forces in the Pacific. On April 19 the southwest Pacific command of the United Nations came into final being. It included the United States, the United Kingdom, Australia, and the Netherlands. New Zealand was technically separated by being included in the simultaneously created south Pacific command under Admiral Chester W. Nimitz. The Australian government, in an official statement, assigned to the supreme commander, MacArthur, all combat sections of the Australian defensive forces and instructed all Australian commanders to consider orders issued by the supreme commander as emanating from the Commonwealth government. The aim of the new command was, the statement concluded, to weld the Australian and American forces into one homo-

[48] *New York Times*, March 31, 1942; *London Times*, April 1, 1942.
[49] The President also remarked that Australia's wish to become a partner in the Munitions Assignment, Shipping, and other boards would not be granted. *New York Times*, April 1, 1942.
[50] *Current Notes*, xiii:57 (1942).   [51] *New York Times*, March 18, 1942.

geneous army. General Sir Thomas Blamey became commander of all United Nations land forces in Australia and United Nations officers were freely intermingled among the various staffs of the supreme command.[52]

Thus within four months after Pearl Harbor the over-all organization of the Pacific war had been established. The initiative had largely come from Australia and the Commonwealth government could well be proud of its diplomatic achievements, which benefited not only Australians but the Allied cause.[53] Once the machinery was created, the greater task of using it successfully against the enemy remained. America necessarily had to perform the major part of this task, but within the limits of physical possibility Australia contributed its full share. Australia lived up to Evatt's assurance that the country would not "creep into safety" behind America's immense power, but would, in cooperation with the United States, fight until the enemy was defeated.[54]

Just as mutual aid between the two nations in the field of supplies had begun long before a legal and organizational framework had been built, so in the sphere of military activity the troops of the two Allies operated conjointly almost immediately after Pearl Harbor. General George C. Marshall, chief of staff of the United States Army, attested to the support America received from Australia. He wrote: "The support and cooperation furnished the United States by the Australian Government and the people has been a vital factor in the conduct of the war in the Far East. All possible assistance was offered to the American commanders in that area in building up the air and supply bases and facilitating the establishment of troop units."[55]

The first American troops reached Australia on December 22, 1941, diverted from their original destination, the Philippines. Soon afterward the first squadrons of the American air force landed, and an immense stream of American troops

[52] *New York Times*, April 20, 22, 1942.
[53] *London Times*, April 1, 1942.   [54] *Australia*, I (March 1942).
[55] Marshall, *Biennial Report on the Army*, July 1, 1941, to June 30, 1943, Note 3.

and supplies followed. By March 1942 the Australian government could announce, with obvious satisfaction, that "most substantial" American forces had arrived in Australia.[56] Early in January United States Army headquarters began to function in Australia and attacked the urgent task of coordinating all available forces—American, Australian, and those of other Allies—for the defense of Australia. Troops were distributed over strategic points on the continent and northern Australia was compared to an armed camp. The presence of a strong American air force permitted the patrolling of the approaches to Australia's coast and as early as March the American and Australian air forces cooperated in bombing attacks upon the Japanese invasion fleets on New Guinea bases.[57] These activities were merely a forerunner of later activities on a much larger scale, encompassing all branches of the armed forces.

As yet the tide of Japanese advances into southeastern Asia and in the direction of Australia was not stemmed. An over-all strategy had still to be mapped out; more American assistance had to be provided; Australian troops, spread all over the battle fronts of Africa, Europe, and Asia, were expected to return; and American and Australian forces had yet to be combined into one striking force. The goal was not simply to protect Australia from invasion, but, as the Australian army minister, Forde, stated, to weld the American and Australian forces into one great army for an offensive, not a defensive, policy.[58]

Perhaps the greatest immediate effect produced by the arrival of American troops in Australia was the tremendous boost in the morale of the Australian people. Observers in Australia seemed agreed that the first reaction of Australians was relief and a stimulus to greater efforts in the knowledge that they would not be alone in withstanding the enemy. American soldiers were prominent in all Australian cities, often outnumbering Australian soldiers, and they received a most cordial welcome. As was to be expected, friction and

---

[56] *New York Times*, March 18, 1942.
[57] *Ibid.*   [58] *Ibid.*, April 5, 1942.

misunderstandings developed at times between American soldiers and local citizens, but on the whole the relations between them were as friendly and close as those between their leaders. Individuals and organizations on both sides did their best to acquaint the two peoples with each other. Within a few months Americans and Australians learned more about each other than they had ever known in the one hundred and fifty years of their existence.[59]

Beginning in the early summer months of 1942, reports of fighting by combined American-Australian forces became frequent. Australian naval forces supported American actions or vice versa. Australian co-pilots could be found in American bombers. American and Australian air squadrons made common sorties and celebrated their first common victory, the Bismarck Sea. On New Guinea American and Australian land forces cooperated for the first time in battle. On November 23, 1942, they joined near Buna, after the Australians had driven the last Japanese back across the Owen Stanley mountains, and after American troops—a colored squadron—had seen their first land action in the Australian area.[60] From then on, the forces of the two nations cooperated as one army in the terrible fighting on New Guinea for many months.

As the war moved into the "island hopping" phase and away from the immediate Australian danger zone, Prime Minister Curtin promised continued participation of Australian troops in the defeat of the enemy "anywhere."[61] And so Australian troops shared the fighting on numerous islands in the spearhead of the Allied armies moving toward Tokyo or engaged in cleaning up by-passed islands. When final victory came, Australian troops could be found in many parts of the Pacific—in New Guinea, the Solomons, the Philippines, the Netherlands Indies. American and Australian troops had established an "invincible comradeship in arms."[62]

[59] Periodicals of the war period are filled with reports on this development. The bibliography in every issue of the Australian News and Information Bureau's publication *Australia* is very complete.

[60] *Australia*, November 1942.

[61] *New York Times*, October 2, 1943.

[62] Curtin, *New York Times*, September 19, 1943.

CHAPTER XII

The New Pacific

THE war brought to America and Australia the completion of developments that had their roots in the middle of the last century. United States power and influence are now firmly spread over all the Pacific. Australia is conducting a policy greatly independent from that of Great Britain. The Pacific war, furthermore, made both nations realize that each is more significant to the other than was believed even in the pre-Pearl Harbor days when arrangements for cooperation were made.

The 150-year-old confidence of Australia in the protection of the British fleet has been rudely shaken. The long passivity of Australia in the conduct of its foreign affairs is definitely at an end. Nor is the Commonwealth willing to live any longer at the "circumference of western civilization."[1] The Australian people are aware that on their part this implies provision for their own protection and that an indispensable element in a system of protection is the existence of a foreign policy made in Australia for Australians. With this idea in mind Australia and New Zealand concluded an agreement at Canberra in January 1944 that expresses the determination of these two nations to have a voice of their own in world affairs and especially in matters affecting the southern and western Pacific. The message contained in the agreement is directed at Great Britain as well as any other power with interests in the Pacific.[2]

The Australian people believe that they have acquired the right to be heard through the great sacrifices they made in the successful prosecution of World War II. The war and

NOTE: Some sections of this chapter appeared first under the title of "Australian Security," in *Dalhousie Review*, xxv:265ff (1945) and *Fortnightly*, CMXLVII (n.s.):328 (1945).

[1] *Current Notes*, xv:20 (1944).

[2] *Ibid.*, 2ff.

their war effort, they claim, have turned Australia into a "great nation," which has definite, vital interests and responsibilities in the Pacific. They consider it their mission to act as trustees of the world—together with New Zealand—in their part of the globe and to apply the principles of freedom from want, fear, and suppression to the countries of the south and southwest Pacific. Indeed, some Australians believe that they have achieved in the southern hemisphere a position comparable to that of the United States in the world, and they therefore demand an equal voice in the councils which will control the destiny of the nations in the world in general and in the Pacific in particular.[3]

The results of these convictions have already become apparent. At the San Francisco Conference in 1945 Australia rejected the role of a small power and demanded "middle power" status. On the occasion of the armistice with Japan, Evatt accused Great Britain of denying equality to Australia in the surrender negotiations. London was bluntly reminded of the changes that had taken place in the empire during the war and that "centralization" had become anachronistic. This, it was pointed out somewhat cynically, would also make the loss of Great Britain less dangerous to Australia![4] The assertion of this right to an independent foreign policy continues to surprise, if not to shock, imperialists both in England and in Australia. The Commonwealth government still finds it necessary to deny any intention of separation from the empire. "This practical handling of their [the Dominion's] own affairs does not conflict in any way with, but strengthens the general conception of the British Commonwealth," maintained the prime minister. Besides, he pointed out, Australia is simply making use of the power of full self-government in external affairs that was granted in the imperial conference of 1937 and which is an "indispensable adjunct to Dominion status."[5] But even with the most

[3] *Ibid.*, 13ff, 19ff; *New York Times*, August 5, 1943; J. B. Brigden, *Australia's Part after the War* (International Conciliation No. 398, Boston, 1944), 205ff.

[4] *New York Times*, April 4, August 20, 25, 27, September 8, 1945.

[5] *Current Notes*, xv:19, 30 (1944); cf. *London Times*, January 24, 1944; *Round Table*, March 1944, p. 169.

favorable interpretation from an empire standpoint, many Britons do not wholeheartedly subscribe to the new Australian initiative.

This "unprecedented departure" in empire affairs[6] is also of considerable interest to powers outside the British Commonwealth of Nations. Formerly foreign nations could conduct their relations with Australia largely through London or at least expect a certain coordination of Anglo-Australian policy, but this need no longer be true in the future. The innovation in Australia's foreign affairs is not simply a hangover from war days that may disappear someday. The danger of invasion and the disappointment with British assistance were effective catalysts in bringing about Australia's determination to have a larger share in shaping its foreign relations, but there are a number of indications that Australia will continue along the newly trodden path.

Japan's attack was a milestone in the evolution of Australia's status in the British Commonwealth and the world, at least in Australian minds. The Japanese action and the imminent danger of defeat proved to Australia that its past fears and the policy based thereon were founded on a proper analysis of trends and events. "The premonitions that Australia had in isolation have been justified," remarked the Australian minister in Washington, and the conclusion Australians are drawing is that Australian policy must be independent, restricted only by physical limitations, and assertive.[7]

The American position in the postwar Pacific is by no means as unequivocal. Obviously, American physical might in the ocean is supreme. If power politics continue to dominate international relations, America's political influence in the Pacific will also be supreme and exclusive. But so far, there is no agreement within the United States on the desirability of the Pacific as a "lake under American jurisdiction," or among those who favor American predominance, on the form this supremacy should take. Opinion is very much

[6] *Observer*, January 23, 1944.
[7] *Current Notes*, XVI:3 (1945); cf. *ibid.*, XVII:146 (1946).

divided both among the public and within the government as to what road America should choose. At the most, it can be said that the United States will play a more important part in Pacific affairs than ever before and that indications point toward establishment of considerable political and economic control; in other words, the tendency is toward making the Pacific an American lake.

Thus the United States and Australia have emerged from the war with a far greater awareness of being "Pacific powers" than they ever had before in their history. Consequently each nation insists more adamantly on what it considers a necessary national Pacific policy. From this situation, differences of opinion have developed already, finding expression mainly in two major problems, the future of Japan and the disposal of Pacific islands.

In the handling of the Japanese situation, friction between Canberra and Washington developed from the very beginning. The Australian attitude is that in the Pacific Australia is a principal power, with interests and rights second only to the United States. As far as the matter of security is concerned, Australia believes that nobody is as vitally concerned in the future arrangements of the Pacific as Australia itself. Australia claims, therefore, the right not only to be consulted but actively to participate in Pacific affairs. The Commonwealth government made this attitude abundantly clear long before the war ended and has ever since been acutely sensitive to any deviation from this principle by any power.[8]

When the time for Japan's surrender arrived, General Blamey participated in the preparations for the great event, but was unable to make arrangements which satisfied the Australian government. The original plan was to have the supreme commander sign for the four big Allied powers and to have these powers represented at the signing and indorse the supreme commander's signature. Australia protested against such an arrangement in London and Washington, and after some skirmishes the State Department finally in-

[8] *Current Notes*, xvi:170 (1945), xvii:21 (1946); *New York Times*, August 14, 20, 1945.

formed General MacArthur that Australia as well as other countries directly concerned in the war against Japan would sign the surrender instrument.[9] A similar arrangement was made for the presence of Australian troops at the surrender of Japanese armies in the southeast Asiatic area. In Foreign Minister Evatt's words, Australia would not be "brushed aside."[10]

In the making of the armistice terms Australia again felt slighted. Immediately upon receiving information from Great Britain that the Allied powers were considering armistice terms for Japan, the Australian government made known in London and other capitals its view that the emperor should be held responsible for Japanese aggression and war crimes. However, the Australian message came too late to be fully considered and the armistice terms did not establish the emperor's responsibility.[11] The Commonwealth government again made clear its standpoint on the desired treatment of Japan. It disagreed with the preservation of the emperor's position. It insisted that the imperial and militarist system and the economic dictatorship of the few great concerns should be abolished, and a complete reformation of Japan's internal structure brought about. Canberra felt, however, that these suggestions and proposals were not adequately considered by the big powers.[12] They differed from the official American view to some degree, though not much in principle. The Australians obviously desired a "tougher" peace for Japan's ruling cliques than Washington seemed willing to make, and the Australian government and press did not hesitate to publicize their dissatisfaction with the treatment they received from the big powers, notwithstanding the fact that President Truman asked them to have patience.[13]

After Japan's surrender on September 2, 1945, the southwest Pacific command came to an end. The forces of each

[9] *Ibid.*, August 18, 1945; *Current Notes*, xvi:173 (1945); xvii:135 (1946).
[10] *Ibid.*, xvi:174 (1945); *New York Times*, November 28, 1945.
[11] *Current Notes*, xvi:169 (1945).
[12] *Ibid.*, 170.
[13] *Ibid.; New York Times*, August 20, 21, September 8, 13, 1945.

Ally returned to its respective government. The Pacific
area was divided into a southeast Asia command and a southwest Pacific area, extending roughly south of the Philippines
and east of Borneo, in which initially Australia accepted responsibility for the surrender of Japanese troops. Eventually, troops of other nationalities took over from the Australians
in much of the territory of the southwest Pacific area. Australia will retain full responsibility, military and civil, over
Papua and Australian mandates.[14]

From the moment of surrender Australia expressed the
desire for participation in the occupation of Japan with a
distinct Australian force under an Australian commander.
In August Canberra announced that a naval, land, and air
force had been assigned to occupation duty in Japan by
Australia "as a separate belligerent" and that the composite
force would have "the same status as the occupation forces
being supplied by the United States, Britain, China, and the
Union of Soviet Socialist Republics."[15] (China and Russia
did not send any occupation troops to Japan.)

On January 31, 1946, an agreement between the United
States and Australia was announced regarding British Commonwealth occupation forces for Japan. In the discussions
leading up to this agreement Australia had been chosen as
the spokesman for the empire and Australia's position in the
occupation arrangement was a very prominent one—a clear
indication that the empire recognized Australia's foremost
interest in the Pacific. The empire force is composed of various branches of the armies of Great Britain, Australia, New
Zealand, and India under the command of an Australian
officer, who is responsible for matters affecting policy and
administration of the empire force to the "Joint Chiefs of
Staff in Australia," created for the purpose. On major policies
affecting the operational capabilities of the force, he has direct
access to the commander in chief, General MacArthur, under
whose supreme command the empire force is placed in Japan.

[14] *Current Notes*, xvi:174ff.
[15] *Ibid.*, 171.

In matters of governmental concern the Australian government acts as representative for the Commonwealth governments. Although the empire force is a distinct military unit, the area it occupies is not a national zone but an integral part of the American military government.[16]

Parallel to these military arrangements for the surrender and control of Japan, the Allies were faced with the task of devising and executing a common policy toward Japan in political, economic, and financial matters pursuant to the surrender terms. The Australian government felt that the Council of Foreign Ministers was incapable of handling this task. Besides, Australia had always advocated that all countries which had a prominent part in the defeat of Japan should participate at the highest level in the formulation of a postwar policy toward Japan.[17] With this plan in mind Foreign Minister Evatt had frequent conversations with Foreign Secretaries Byrnes and Bevin in London, just before the first meeting of the Council of Foreign Ministers. His activity was partly responsible for the decision of the big four powers to create the Far Eastern Advisory Commission, which was announced October 11, 1945. The Australian government was satisfied that the commission was a step forward in the direction of unified control of Japan: Foreign Minister Evatt called it "an experiment of a democratic kind in consultation and cooperation by the Pacific countries that fought the war against Japan."[18] His enthusiasm was soon dampened.

The commission had ten members: Great Britain, China, the United States, France, Australia, New Zealand, India, Canada, the Netherlands, and the Philippines. In accordance with its assumed role of defender of the rights of small powers, Australia insisted in the very first meeting of the commission, when its constitution and powers were vague, that all members should be consulted on and have full par-

<hr>

[16] *Ibid.*, xvii:27 (1946); U.S. Department of State, *Bulletin*, xiv:220 (1946).

[17] *Current Notes*, xvii:19ff (1946); *New York Times*, September 8, 1945. Werner Levi, "International Control of Japan," *Far Eastern Survey*, xv:299 (1946).

[18] *Ibid.*, October 12, 28, 1945; *Current Notes*, xvii:19ff, 134 (1946).

ticipation in any amendments of the constitution or determination of the terms of reference of the commission. However, the United States government disagreed and finally announced officially that it "is not consulting with any Governments other than Russia, China and France of the Far Eastern Advisory Commission. Other interested Governments will of course be kept informed of these consultations and in the particular case of the request made by the Australian representative on the Commission, it is assumed that the British Government will consult with all the Dominion Governments represented on the Commission." Evatt's answer to this was the following statement: "At the first meeting of the Commission the representatives of Australia and France speaking with the implied approval of other representatives requested adequate consultation before any new proposals for the powers and functions of the Commission were finalized. If so reasonable a request is rejected it is a poor outlook for that international co-operation which is always preached and not always practised. Under United States leadership Australia's contribution to victory in the Pacific was sustained without pause and without stint from Pearl Harbour right up to the day of final victory. As a matter of justice this war effort should carry with it the undoubted right of full and timely consultation on the basis of partnership and comradeship in all that concerns the carrying out of the Japanese armistice and the making of the peace. This is Australia's claim and we shall never abandon it."[19] The Australians were also dissatisfied with the veto right of the big powers in the commission, which of course further reduced the influence of the smaller nations.

During the meeting of the Council of Foreign Ministers in Moscow in December 1945, the Far Eastern Advisory Commission was replaced by a Far Eastern Commission with its seat in Washington and an Allied Council for Japan, with the seat in Tokyo. The membership of the new commission and council was increased by Russia's accession. The juris-

---

[19] *Ibid.*, XVI:221 (1945); *New York Times*, October 31, 1945.

diction of the commission was enlarged. Generally, the task of the commission is to formulate broad policies for the handling of Japan, while the supreme commander, who retains a considerable amount of discretion, is to execute these policies. The council is essentially a consultative and advisory body.[20] Again, the big four retain a veto power, much to the disappointment of the Australian government. Evatt maintained that the veto power was undemocratic and indefensible and would "ruin the good work" of the commission, and lodged a protest with the United States government.[21] Besides, he felt that the veto power in addition to the discretionary power left to General MacArthur would give the United States an undue share of control over all measures in regard to Japan.[22]

On the whole, Australia is pleased that its claim to an important status in the Pacific has found recognition—in the appointment of prominent Australians as commander of the empire occupation force, as empire representative to the Allied council in Tokyo, and as president of the Allied tribunal for the prosecution of Japanese war criminals.[23] But there still is dissatisfaction, especially with the United States, with the subordinate role which the big powers have assigned to Australia in an area which that nation considers of vital importance to its existence.

The second major problem, the disposal of Pacific island bases, is also unsolved as yet. Here again Australia has more definite plans than the United States.[24] The major Australian policy is outlined in the Canberra agreement of 1944. It calls for the creation of a regional defense zone within a general system of world security. For obvious reasons Australia does not attempt to devise a system for world security but it has very definite ideas on the shape of the regional defense system. A security zone is to have its base in Australia and New

[20] For text see *Current Notes*, xvii:24ff (1946).
[21] *Ibid.*, 26, 138; *New York Times*, January 8, 1946.
[22] Cf. *ibid.*, November 17, 1945.   [23] *Current Notes*, xvii:92, 136 (1946).
[24] Werner Levi, "The United States and Pacific Bases," *Fortnightly*, cmlvii (n.s.):165 (1946).

Zealand and is to extend through the arc of islands north and northeast of Australia to western Samoa and the Cook Islands. The Commonwealth government is willing to share in the policing of such areas of the south and southwest Pacific as may be assigned to it within the framework of a world security system. This regional system is to be integrated into the world system and, it is hoped, will provide security for Australia even if a world system should fail. At the San Francisco Conference and ever since, Australia has been an outstanding advocate of regional security systems.

The Canberra agreement states specifically that the establishment of military installations by one power in any territory belonging to another power does not establish a claim to such territory. This is a clear expression, often since repeated by Commonwealth statesmen, that Australia is opposed to the United States' claiming outright possession to islands now under the sovereignty of one of the Allies by mere right of conquest. Canberra believes that changes of sovereignty over islands belonging to any Ally are not a matter of right but of discussion at the peace table on the basis of reciprocity. Lately the Australian government seems to include the formerly Japanese mandated islands in this principle.[25] There is uneasiness in Australia over this problem, the more so because Australians realize their dependence on stronger nations for security, yet dislike to see any power, even a most friendly one, established in the northern approaches to their country.[26]

The Australian attitude toward defense in the Pacific was resented by some American congressmen as a restriction upon American freedom of action. The Canberra agreement was characterized as an unkind and most disturbing act indicating that Australia and New Zealand were planning to dominate the south and southwest Pacific. It was considered a move affecting the legitimate postwar aims and aspirations of the United States, its security, and its share in air and sea

[25] *New York Times,* April 25, August 15, 1944; *Current Notes,* xvII:147 (1946).

[26] *New York Times,* September 8, 1945, April 25, 1946.

trade routes in the Pacific area.[27] No amount of denial by Australian and New Zealand officials was able to disperse these suspicions altogether, which in the face of Australian realities seemed groundless. The agreement was ascribed sufficient importance to provoke action in Congress.

A twenty-one man "Select Committee on Post-War Military Policy" was created in the House, whose main task was to chart a program for the disposal of Pacific island bases.[28] From the President down, various American officials from civilian and military branches of the government made statements regarding the future of these island bases. These statements ranged from assurances that the United States would not annex any territory to demands that the government simply take whatever was believed necessary for the security of the country.[29] There does not appear to be any agreement within the government on a definite policy. Persons connected directly or indirectly with the Navy are in the forefront of those asking for the acquisition of island bases and American policy and public opinion seem to be tending in that direction, possibly because of the comparative silence of those disapproving of such a program. The most inclusive statement in favor of the American acquisition of bases in some form came from a subcommittee on Pacific bases of the Committee on Naval Affairs in the House of Representatives in August 1945.[30]

A report from this committee reached the following conclusions: The United States should have "dominating control" over the Marshall, Carolina, Mariana, Izu, Bonin, and Ryukyu islands. The United States should be given "specific and substantial" rights to sites where American bases have been constructed on island territories of Allied nations. The United States should have full title to bases on islands mandated to or claimed by other nations, because these nations

[27] *Ibid.*, March 9, April 19, 1944.
[28] *Congressional Record*, March 3, 1944, p. 2280; March 8, 1944, p. 2427; March 28, 1944, p. 3247; *New York Times*, March 9, 1944.
[29] For details see Levi, "Australian Security," *passim.*
[30] For the text of the report, see *United States News*, August 24, 1945.

are incapable of defending such bases and because these bases are vital links in the American chain of security. American bases should be permanently kept in a state of preparedness.

The Pacific strategy of defense should revolve about a center line north of the equator to Hawaii, Micronesia, and the Philippines. This line should be protected north and south by certain major bases, secondary bases, fleet anchorages, and airfields. All islands on which bases are situated should become economically self-supporting as far as the native population is concerned, and the natives should be Americanized without a simultaneous destruction of their cultural characteristics. In peacetime the bases should be used for commercial shipping and air lines.

These conclusions were based on the assumption that the United Nations Charter would be signed, that the United States would take over the task of preserving peace in the Pacific, that this task requires adequate bases, and that the American fleet would be maintained superior to that of any "probable" aggressor.

The report gives as reasons justifying these broad American claims American security, security of the western hemisphere, Pacific peace, sacrifice of American lives on the islands, American development of the islands, and the desire of the natives for American control. Whether or not these arguments can withstand a critical analysis, they are effective and widely held among sections of the American people. Although the report is described by the authors as incomplete and preliminary and was written before the arrival of the atomic bomb, subsequent utterances by responsible persons inside and outside the government indicate that its ideas are not outmoded. The armed forces are proceeding with the fortification of a number of Pacific islands and the Navy Department has submitted to the Senate atomic energy committee a list of fifty-two islands which it considers essential for American security.[31] Among these islands are the Manus, which belong to the Australian mandate of the Admiralty

[31] *New York Times*, February 24, 1946.

group, and conversations between Washington and Canberra over the American acquisition of the Manus have been inaugurated.[32]

The American and the Australian plan for the disposal of Pacific island bases cannot be reconciled without some concessions on both sides. The Atlantic Charter would prevent the United States from annexing any territory, since this would amount to territorial aggrandizement. The most likely choice of the American government will be exclusive trusteeship over the desired island bases, although some congressmen are opposed to anything short of outright annexation.[33] To this, Australia will not agree. The Commonwealth government again made clear during the empire conference in London in the spring of 1946 that it will resist any American demand for the sovereign retention of islands situated in territories under British, Australian, or New Zealand mandate.[34]

However, in the recognition that Australia's security cannot be safeguarded without American assistance, Australian public and official opinion favors America's increasing influence in the Pacific. Since the beginning of the war, public opinion polls showed that Australians were glad to grant the United States the use of bases even on Australian territory and, to judge by press opinion, Australians are still willing—in peacetime—to let the United States maintain a strong base on the Manus or any other Pacific island, provided that this is done by mutual agreement. They consider such an arrangement a measure of self-protection.[35]

To Australians the ideal solution of the Pacific island problem, one which would provide the desired security, yet avoid the monopolization of bases close to Australia by any one power, would be a regional agreement among all Pacific powers, by which each of these powers would be responsible for a given zone—with part of the United States zone within

[32] *Ibid.*, February 16, 1946.
[33] *Ibid.*, January 16, 17, 31, 1946.
[34] *London Sunday Times,* April 28, 1946.
[35] *New York Times,* April 25, May 6, May 10, 1946.

the Australian-administered area—but by which the defense plans of all powers would be dovetailed and each would give access to its bases to the other.[36] Foreign Minister Evatt summed up Australia's stand as follows: "The Government will enter into no commitments which will lessen the control of the Australian people over their own territories. Any consideration of plans for the joint use of any bases in Australia's dependent territories should be preceded by an over-all defence arrangement for the region of the Western Pacific, including the islands formerly mandated to Japan; as an incident of any such arrangement, Australia should be entitled to reciprocal use of foreign bases in the region, thus providing for an over-all increase in the security both of Australia and of all other United Nations with interests in the region.

"The detailed means of implementing a security policy for the Pacific have yet to be decided, but this much is already apparent: Australian security is very largely dependent on our closest co-operation with the British Commonwealth and the United States of America. Any hindrance to the maximum degree of co-operation with either is contrary to the interests of all these countries. It should be added that regional arrangements for defence are not only permitted but encouraged by the Charter so long as the objectives are in accordance with the principles of the United Nations."[37]

The most authoritative reaction to this regional security plan came from Admiral Leahy, chief of staff to President Truman, who maintained that there were "no difficulties whatever to a complete agreement by both parties" on the island question.[38] Some newspaper reports from Washington and London were less optimistic.

Differences in policy on the Pacific bases, a long delay in replacing the departed American minister in Canberra, and friction over the establishment of civilian airlines between

[36] *Australia*, IV (January 1945); *Chicago Daily Tribune*, May 4, 1945; *New York Times*, November 17, 1945, April 25, May 6, 1946; *London Sunday Times*, April 28, 1946.

[37] *Current Notes*, XVII:147 (1946).

[38] *New York Times*, May 18, August 5, 1946; *Sydney Morning Herald*, June 22, July 11, 1946.

Australia and the United States have led some Australians to doubt the depth of friendship between the two nations. The *Sydney Morning Herald* spoke of a "chilling of the warm friendship." This elicited immediate denials from high officials in both countries; the elevation of the American and Australian legations in Canberra and Washington to the rank of embassies in July 1946 is proof of the mutual friendship and respect of both nations.[89]

Experience during the war has shown that the United States and Australia are important to each other and that the security of both depends to a considerable degree on cooperation. Since the policy of neither nation indicates its conviction that the United Nations will eliminate the need for mutual or regional security agreements, realism on both sides will make possible a compromise solution on the island question and other problems, and thus enable the two nations to be of mutual assistance.

[89] *Ibid.*, July 11, 16, 1946; U.S. Dept. of State, *Bulletin*, July 1946.

Bibliography

I. MANUSCRIPTS

The papers of Admiral Charles S. Sperry. Manuscript Division, Library of Congress.

II. OFFICIAL DOCUMENTS

Australia

Department of External Affairs, *Current Notes on International Affairs.*
Official Year Book of the Commonwealth of Australia (Annual).
Parliament of Australia, Joint Library Committee, *Historical Records of Australia, 1914– .*
Parliamentary Debates.
Parliamentary Papers, LXI, No. 2, *Conference on the Limitation of Armament, Report of the Australian Delegate.* Melbourne.

Germany

Die Grosse Politik der Europaeischen Kabinette. Berlin, 1921–1927.

Great Britain

Bigge, John Thomas, *Report of the Commissioner of Inquiry on the State of Agriculture and Trade in the Colony of New South Wales.* London, 1823.
Conference of the Prime Ministers and Representatives of the United Kingdom, the Dominions, and India, Cmd. 1474. London, 1921.
Gooch, G. P., and H. W. V. Temperley, eds. *British Documents on the Origins of the World War, 1898–1914.* London, 1926–1938.
Hansard, *Parliamentary Debates.*
House of Commons, *Journal.*
Imperial Conference 1923, Cmd. 1987. London, 1923.

League of Nations

Official Journal.

New South Wales

Historical Records of New South Wales. Sydney, 1893–1901.
Parliament, Legislative Council, *The Speeches in the Legislative Council of New South Wales on the Second Reading of the Bill for Framing a New Constitution for the Colony.* Sydney, 1853.
Statistical Returns, 1841–1850; 1837–1852. Sydney.

Queensland

Parliamentary Debates.

United States

Conference on the Limitation of Armament, Senate Document No. 126, 67th Congress, 2nd Session (1922).
Congressional Globe.
Congressional Record.
Department of State:
  Bulletin.
  Consular Dispatches, Melbourne.
  Consular Dispatches, Sydney.
  Papers Relating to the Foreign Relations of the United States, 1883– .
  Papers Relating to the Foreign Relations of the United States, Japan 1931–1941 (1943).
  Papers Relating to the Foreign Relations of the United States, Paris Peace Conference 1919 (1942–).
Department of the Navy:
  Official Records of the Union and Confederate Navies in the War of the Rebellion, 1896.
Department of War:
  Marshall, George C., *Biennial Reports on the Army.*
Hasse, A. R., *Index to United States Documents Relating to Foreign Affairs*, 1921.
House Document No. 179, 20th Congress, 1st Session (1828).
House Executive Document No. 161, 44th Congress, 1st Session (May 1, 1876).
President's *Twentieth Report to Congress on Lend-Lease Operations*. Washington, August 30, 1945.
Report of the Postmaster General, House Executive Document No. 1, Pt. 4, 42nd Congress, 2nd Session (November 18, 1871) and 3rd Session (November 15, 1872).
Report of the Secretary of the Navy, House Executive Document No. 1, 40th Congress, 3rd Session (December 7, 1868).
Report of the Senate Committee on Naval Affairs, No. 194, 40th Congress, 3rd Session (January 28, 1869).
Senate Report No. 316, 41st Congress, 3rd Session (January 26, 1871).
Stettinius, Edward R., Jr., *Report to the 78th Congress on Lend-Lease Operations* (January 25, 1943).

Victoria

Federation, and Foreign Convicts. Melbourne, 1884.
Parliamentary Debates.

III. BOOKS

Alexander, Fred. *Australia and the United States*. Boston, 1941.
Australian Handbook. Sydney, 1889.
Australian Institute of International Affairs. *Australia and the Pacific*. Princeton, 1944.
Baker, Ray Stannard. *What Wilson Did at Paris*. New York, 1919.
Ball, W. Macmahon, ed. *Press, Radio, and World Affairs*. Melbourne, 1928.
Battye, James S. *Western Australia*. Oxford, 1924.
Bentham, Jeremy. *A Plea for the Constitution . . .* London, 1803.

Bisson, Thomas A. *America's Far Eastern Policy*. New York, 1945.

Bond, Phineas. "Letters." *Annual Report of the American Historical Association*, 1896.

Bonsal, Stephen. *Unfinished Business*. New York, 1944.

Brigden, J. B. *Australia's Part after the War*. International Conciliation No. 398. Boston, 1944.

Brookes, Jean Ingram. *International Rivalry in the Pacific Islands, 1800–1875*. Berkeley, 1941.

Callahan, James Morton. *American Relations in the Pacific and Far East, 1784–1900*. Baltimore, 1901.

Chatterton, E. Keble. *Whalers and Whaling*. London, 1924.

Clark, Arthur H. *The Clipper Ship Era*. New York, 1910.

Coggeshall, George. *History of the American Privateers*. New York, 1856.

Cole, Percival R. *The United States and Australia*. International Conciliation No. 28, Supplement. New York, 1910.

Copland, Douglas B. *Australia in the World Crisis, 1929–1933*. New York, 1934.

Daniel, Howard, and Minnie Belle. *Australia, The New Customer*. New York, 1946.

Delano, Alonzo. *Across the Plains and Among the Diggings*. New York, 1936.

Dennett, Tyler. *Americans in Eastern Asia*. New York, 1941.

Dennis, Alfred L. P. *Adventures in American Diplomacy*. New York, 1928.

Dietrich, Ethel B. *Far Eastern Trade of the United States*. New York, 1940.

Dunbabin, Thomas. *The Making of Australasia*. London, 1922.

Duncan, W. G. K., ed. *Australia's Foreign Policy*. Sydney, 1938.

Elliott, William Yandell, and H. Duncan Hall, eds. *The British Commonwealth at War*. New York, 1943.

Erskine, John E. *Journal of a Cruise Among the Islanders of the Western Pacific*. London, 1853.

Fanning, Edmund. *Voyages and Discoveries in the South Seas, 1792–1832*. Salem, 1924.

Fitzmaurice, Edmond. *Life of Granville*. 2 vols. London, 1905.

Fitzpatrick, Brian. *The British Empire in Australia*. Melbourne, 1941.

Flanagan, Roderick. *The History of New South Wales*. 2 vols. London, 1862.

Gerig, Benjamin. *The Open Door and the Mandates System*. London, 1930.

Grattan, C. Hartley. *Introducing Australia*. New York, 1942.

Greenwood, Gordon. *Early American-Australian Relations*. Melbourne, 1944.

Grey, Edward, Viscount of Fallodon. *Twenty-Five Years, 1892–1916*. 2 vols. New York, 1925.

Griffin, Eldon. *Clippers and Consuls*. Ann Arbor, 1938.

Griswold, A. Whitney. *The Far Eastern Policy of the United States*. New York, 1938.

Hall, Henry L. *Australia and England*. London, 1934.

Hargraves, Edward H. *Australia and its Gold Fields*. London, 1855.

Harris, Harold Lark. *Australia's National Interests and National Policy*. Melbourne, 1928.

Howay, Frederick W., ed. *Voyages of the "Columbia" to the Northwest Coast*. Boston, 1941.

Heaton, Herbert. *The British Way to Recovery*. Minneapolis, 1934.

Hughes, William Morris. *The Splendid Adventure*. London, 1929.

Hunt, Cornelius E. *The Shenandoah*. New York, 1867.

Hunt, Erling M. *American Precedents in Australian Federation.* New York, 1930.

Jose, Arthur W. *Builders and Pioneers of Australia.* London, 1928.

Kawakami, Kiyoshi K. *Japan's Pacific Policy.* New York, 1922.

Latourette, Kenneth S. "Early Relations between the United States and China." *Transactions* of the Connecticut Academy of Arts and Science, XXI (1917).

Lloyd George, David. *Memoirs of the Peace Conference.* 2 vols. New Haven, 1939.

———— *War Memoirs.* 6 vols. London, 1934.

Mackaness, George. *Admiral Arthur Phillip.* Sydney, 1937.

Massary, Isabel. *Social Life and Manners in Australia.* London, 1861.

Melbourne, Alexander C. V. *Early Constitutional Development in Australia.* London, 1934.

Merens, Henri. *Etude sur les colonies Anglaises Autonomes de l'Australie et du Canada.* Toulouse, 1907.

Miller, David H. *My Diary at the Peace Conference.* New York, 1924.

Moore, John Bassett. *A Digest of International Law.* 8 vols. Washington, 1906.

———— *Four Phases of American Development, Federalism, Democracy, Imperialism, Expansion.* Baltimore, 1912.

Muir, Ramsay. *A Short History of the British Commonwealth.* 2 vols. New York, 1924.

Murdoch, Walter. *Alfred Deakin.* London, 1923.

Ogle, Nathaniel. *The Colony of Western Australia.* London, 1839.

Paton, John G. *An Autobiography.* 2 vols. New York, 1889.

Pitkin, Timothy. *A Statistical View of the Commerce of the United States of America.* New York, 1817.

Porter, David. *Journal of a Cruise to the Pacific Ocean.* Philadelphia, 1815.

———— *A Voyage to the South Seas in the Years 1812–1814.* London, 1823.

Putnam, George Granville. *Salem Vessels and their Voyages.* Salem, 1930.

Quigley, Harold S. *Far Eastern War, 1937–1941.* Boston, 1942.

Quigley, Harold S., and George H. Blakeslee. *The Far East.* Boston, 1938.

Quincy, Josiah, ed. *The Journals of Major Samuel Shaw.* Boston, 1847.

Rappard, William E. *The Quest for Peace.* Cambridge, Mass., 1940.

Rose, J. Holland, Arthur P. Newton, and E. A. Beneans, eds. *The Cambridge History of the British Empire.* 7 vols. Cambridge, 1933.

Read, Georgia Willis, and Ruth Gaines, eds. *Gold Rush.* 2 vols. New York, 1944.

Ross, I. Clunies, ed. *Australia and the Far East.* Sydney, 1936.

Ryden, George H. *The Foreign Policy of the United States in Relation to Samoa.* New Haven, 1933.

Sanderson, John. *Biography of the Signers to the Declaration of Independence.* Philadelphia, 1828.

Scholefield, Guy H. *The Pacific, Its Past and Future.* London, 1919.

Scott, Ernest. *Short History of Australia.* Oxford, 1927.

———— *Terre Napoléon.* London, 1910.

Seymour, Charles, ed. *The Intimate Papers of Colonel House.* 4 vols. Boston, 1926.

Shann, Edward. *An Economic History of Australia.* Cambridge, 1930.

Shepherd, Jack. *Australia's Interests and Policies in the Far East.* New York, 1940.

Soulé, Frank, and others. *The Annals of San Francisco.* New York, 1855.

Stettinius, Edward R. *Lend-Lease.* New York, 1944.

Strabolgi, Lord Joseph M. K. *Singapore and After*. London, 1942.

Taussig, Charles W. *Rum, Romance and Rebellion*. New York, 1928.

Temperley, Harold W. V., ed. *A History of the Peace Conference*. 6 vols. London, 1924.

Therry, Roger. *Reminiscences of Thirty Years' Residence in New South Wales and Victoria*. London, 1863.

Thompson, Lindsay G. *History of the Fisheries of New South Wales*. Sydney, 1893.

Tilby, A. Wyatt. *Australasia, 1688–1911*. Boston, 1912.

Train, George Francis. *An American Merchant in Europe, Asia, and Australia*. New York, 1857.

Trevelyan, George M. *Grey of Fallodon*. Boston, 1937.

Turner, Henry G. *A History of the Colony of Victoria*. London, 1904.

Walker, Eric A. *The British Empire*. London, 1943.

Weeden, William B. "Early Oriental Commerce in Providence." *Proceedings* of the Massachusetts Historical Society, 3rd session.

Wentworth, W. C. *Statistical, Historical and Political Description of New South Wales*. London, 1819.

Wilkes, Charles. *Narrative of the United States Exploring Expedition*. Philadelphia, 1845.

Willard, Myra. *History of the White Australia Policy*. Melbourne, 1923.

Williams, Mary Floyd. *History of the San Francisco Committee of Vigilance of 1851*. Berkeley, 1921.

Williams, Mary Floyd, ed. *Papers of the San Francisco Committee of Vigilance of 1851*. Berkeley, 1919.

Windett, Nancy M. *Australia as Producer and Trader, 1920–1932*. Oxford, 1933.

IV. ARTICLES

Atkinson, Meredith. "The Washington Conference. Australia's Position." *Nineteenth Century*, xc:941–49 (1921).

"Australia's Mandates." *New Statesman*, xvi:724 (1920).

"An Australian View of Mr. Hughes in Paris." *New Statesman*, xiv:399–400 (1920).

Bates, George H. "Some Aspects of the Samoan Question." *Century Magazine*, xv (n.s.):945–49 (1889).

Belshaw, James P. "Markets for Australian Exports." *Far Eastern Survey*, xiv:58–62 (1945).

Blakeslee, George H. "Japan's Island Possessions in the Pacific." *Journal of International Relations*, xii:173–91 (1921–22).

Brebner, J. B. "Canada, the Anglo-Japanese Alliance and the Washington Conference." *Political Science Quarterly*, l:45–58 (1935).

Casey, R. G. "Australia in World Affairs." *Australian National Review*, ii:2–12 (1937).

Churchward, L. G. "Australian-American Relations during the Gold Rush." *Historical Studies—Australia and New Zealand*, ii:11–24 (1942).

Daniel, Howard, and Minnie Belle. "Australia and Lend-Lease." *Far Eastern Survey*, xxii:233–36 (1943).

"Democratic Government in Victoria." *Westminster Review*, lxxxix:225–45 (1868).

Earsman, W. P. "The Pacific in World Politics." *Labour Monthly*, IV:235–43 (1923).

Eggleston, F. W. "Washington and After, an Australian View." *Nineteenth Century*, XCII:455–65 (1922).

Flake, Wilson C. "Australia." *Foreign Commerce Weekly*, XVII:37 (December 16, 1944).

Furber, Holden. "The Beginning of American Trade with India, 1784–1812." *New England Quarterly*, XI:235–65 (1938).

Greenbie, Sydney. "The Pacific Triangle." *North American Review*, CCXL:340–47 (1920).

Jacobs, Alfred. "Les Européens dans l'Océanie." *Revue des deux Mondes*, XIX: 88–119 (1859).

James, A. A. "Australia and the Anglo-U.S. Treaty." *The Fortnightly*, XCLIX: 181–87 (1938).

Jones, Dorsey W. "The Foreign Policy of William Morris Hughes of Australia." *Far Eastern Quarterly*, II:153–62 (1942).

Leigh, John G. "The Powers and Samoa." *The Fortnightly*, LXXI:54–73 (1899).

Levi, Werner. "Australian Security." *Dalhousie Review*, XXV:265–75 (1945) and *The Fortnightly*, CMXLVII (n.s.):328–35 (1945).

——— "International Control of Japan." *Far Eastern Survey*, XV:299–302 (1946).

——— "The United States and Pacific Bases." *The Fortnightly*, CMLVII (n.s.): 165–171 (1946).

Masson, M., and J. F. Jameson. "The Odyssey of Thomas Muir." *American Historical Review*, XXIX:49–72 (1923).

McNamara, Harry. "Australia and the United Nations." *Amerasia*, VII:337–46 (1943).

"Memoir of Elias Hasket Derby, Merchant of Salem, Massachusetts." *Hunt's Merchant Magazine*, XXXVI:173 (1857).

"The New Pacific." *Littel's Living Age*, CCXXIII:262 (1899).

"Papers respecting the Negociation for a Renewal of the East India Company's exclusive Privileges, 1812." *Quarterly Review*, VIII:239–86 (1812).

"Political and Social Prospects of the Australian Colonies." *Fraser's Magazine*, LVII:659–70 (1858).

Reid, George Houston. "The American Fleet in Australia." *North American Review*, CLXXXIX:404–9 (1909).

"Report of the Committee of Correspondence of the East India Company." *The Pamphleteer*, II:94–154 (1813).

Rossiter, W. S. "The First American Imperialist." *North American Review*, CLXXXII:239–54 (1906).

"Some Problems of Australian Policy." *National Review*, XCV:716–32 (1905).

Taylor, H. C. "The Control of the Pacific." *Forum*, III:406–16 (1887).

V. NEWSPAPERS AND PERIODICALS

Occasional references from the following newspapers and periodicals have been used in the text:

Amerasia, American Law Review, Asiatic Journal, L'Asie Française, Australia, The Australian, Australian National Review, British Australasian, Chicago Daily Tribune, The Colonist, Commonweal, The Economist (London), *Edinburgh Re-*

view, *The Empire, Hunt's Merchant Magazine, Illustrated London News, Japan Weekly Chronicle, Japan Weekly Mail, Journal des Economistes, Le Matin* (Paris), *Literary Digest, Living Age, London Courier, London Morning Chronicle, London Observer, London Sunday Times, London Times, Manchester Guardian Weekly, Melbourne Age, Melbourne Argus, Melbourne Herald, Missionary Herald, The Nation, New South Wales Government Gazette, New Statesman and Nation, New York Daily Tribune, New York Herald, New York Times, Niles' Register, The Patriot, Review of Reviews, Revue Britannique, Round Table, Salem Gazette, San Francisco Herald, Sydney Gazette, Sydney Morning Herald, United States News.*

Index